Setting Up &
Operating
a Business
in Japan

Helene Thian

# Setting Up & Operating a Business in Japan

Charles E. Tuttle Company
Rutland, Vermont & Tokyo, Japan

Published by the Charles E. Tuttle Co., Inc.
of Rutland, Vermont and Tokyo, Japan
with editorial offices at
2-6 Suido 1-chome, Bunkyo-ku, Tokyo 112

©1988 by Charles E. Tuttle Co., Inc.

Library of Congress Catalog Card No. 88-50780
International Standard Book No. 0-8048-1544-5

First printing, 1988

Printed in Japan

To:
*Dr. Hewitte A. Thian, entrepreneur par excellence,*
*Colleen C. Thian, entrepreneur sub rosa,*
*and Yoshiaki Sugasawa*

# Contents

# Preface

ONCE, ENTREPRENEURS WENT WEST. Now, the movement seems to be to the East. This book is about those non-Japanese who, as business pioneers, have seen opportunity in Japan and capitalized upon it, which is what enterprising entrepreneurship is all about. Based on interviews with over forty business owners and experts in Japan, this is a handbook for small business hopefuls already in the country or overseas.

As scholar Yamamoto Shichihei has noted, "By the early Tokugawa period (1603–1868), it had become axiomatic that nothing can last very long without economic rationality; no individual, no merchant nor domain could survive, much less succeed, if he ignored the 'logic of capital.'" Foreigners involved in small business in Japan are attuned to the logic of capital and to the particularities of doing business in the Japanese socio-cultural setting. Whether by trial and error, through support organizations, the aid of friends and family, or a combination of these, the small, foreign business has landed and is thriving. It is hoped that documenting the various aspects of these businesses will be educational for the uninitiated seeking to establish a business and for the existing business owner as well. However, much of the information herein is pertinent to any foreign enterprise seeking to set up in Japan.

This is not only a documentary of methodology, but also of perseverance, optimism, and adaptation, the qualities that must be cultivated to succeed in business in Japan.

Why Tokyo? Why Japan? A variety of reasons exists in response to these questions. One European had worked for over eight years in Japan as a representative of a large corporation, then felt that

13

to return to Europe would be like starting from scratch and would waste a chance to utilize his knowledge about Japan. The answer for Dick Adler of Corton Trading was that "there were fewer Americans in Japan than in America."

However, most of those interviewed acknowledged that opportunity is plentiful in Japan, the main reason for coming and for staying after arriving as tourists or corporate representatives. About 50% of the business owners had been expatriate personnel, or had worked for big business as local hire, because they possessed special skills (which ultimately led to their ability to establish an independent business in Japan). The leap from corporate representative or employee to independent businessman usually came after at least five years. Bunny Cramer of Witan Associates, a corporate communications firm, established her offices after working for six years for Canon. She considered herself an expatriate's wife with no inkling that she would remain in Japan as an independent business owner, but due to her accumulation of knowledge during her stay, decided to put up her own shingle. A businessman who owns a profitable pet food import business worked for a large electronics manufacturer for nine years, but was ousted after he had laid the groundwork for increased sales of the company's items. "They decided that they could do it without me, although I had done all the work. So I went out on my own." Since his sales now amount to ¥1 billion annually, venturing out brought better returns.

Hobbies became businesses in a few instances. Claus Regge of Network, Inc. and Soundwork, Inc. started importing orchestral quality oboes because he wanted to provide Japanese artists with the opportunity to purchase fine quality instruments from Europe. Michael Dunn, an art/antique dealer, fell in love with Japan at an early age and after working as a corporate representative in Japan for six years, turned his art collecting hobby into a business, saying, "I wasn't a corporate man."

Two British expatriates, Graham Pike, a shipping lines owner, and Edmund Daszkiewicz, involved in computer software sales, emphasized the lack of job opportunities in their own country as the reason for remaining in Japan. "It was actually a depressing situation," said Daszkiewicz, who worked for a Japanese company for three years before using his expertise in computers and program development in his own venture.

Another prevalent reason for operating a business in Japan was that entrepreneurs had married Japanese citizens, a great help in filling out forms and applications and an invaluable aid to understanding the system. Fran Kuzui of Kuzui Enterprises, an entertainment promotion and film distribution company, married a Japanese, and, as both were working in the film industry, thought it would be natural to set up shop in Japan as well as New York where they had originally started out. Nearly half of the interviewees had Japanese spouses and were appreciative of their help in business endeavors.

A business consultant/lawyer says, "It was being in the right place at the right time or dumb luck." His reasoning is not unusual, but one interviewee's observation rings closer to the real reason for being in Japan. "Japan is where it's at. The market is here and so is a wealth of information."

Whether due to corporate divergence, limited job opportunities at home, political reasons, marriage with a Japanese, a belief in Japan as an unconquered business frontier, or just "dumb luck," small foreign businesses are in Japan and are growing in quantity and variety. As Neil Butler, former President of the Australian Business Association, says, "having a business in Tokyo is exciting, demanding, and difficult—and I like it," sentiments echoed by all of Japan's new, foreign, independent businessmen.

**Note:** Please be aware that although up-to-date at the time of writing, some of the information in this book is subject to change.

# Acknowledgments

To Ms. Victoria A. Fisher for her incomparable brainstorming, mentorship and zeal, *hontō ni, arigatō gozaimashita*.

To Ms. Reiko Lyster for being available 100% of the time, a 200% thank you. To Ms. Bunny Cramer for her encouragement and enthusiasm, a bouquet of appreciation.

To Fukuko Miyata and Shigeko Saito for OA instruction and mechanical assistance, *kansha shimasu*.

To Jonathan Lloyd-Owen for the proper introductions and Jonathan Malamud and Steve Woodsmall for the proper inquiries, *dōmo, dōmo*.

I also wish to sincerely thank every interviewee for the enlightening discourses and for the admirable will to succeed in Japan. This book is a tribute to you and to entrepreneurship.

# Acknowledgments

# 1

# Introduction

## WHAT IS A SMALL BUSINESS?

The definition offered by the U.S. Small Business Administration is as follows: "A company, including all affiliates and subsidiaries worldwide, whose net sales do not exceed $5 million annually and whose combined assets do not exceed $10 million." The definition of the Ministry of International Trade and Industry of Japan (MITI) is preoccupied instead with quantification; that is, if an entity is engaged in wholesale trade and capitalized at ¥30 million or less, or employs 100 workers or less, it is considered a small business. If an entity is engaged in the retail trade and is capitalized at ¥10 million or less or employs 50 workers or less, it is also considered a small business.

Since this book is about businesses in Japan, the MITI definition pertains. However, a small business in Japan more closely corresponds to the American definition, as has been noted by the Small Business Promotion Committee of the American Chamber of Commerce in Japan.

Technical definitions aside, a "small business" is a one- or two-person operation in the beginning, and while the number of personnel may grow over time, 80% of the businesses interviewed for this book were owner-operated with little or no staff.

## WHY START A BUSINESS IN JAPAN?

Having defined the perimeters of the small business, listing the services and products offered by the people interviewed for this book will enable the reader to visualize the niches being created and the needs being fulfilled by foreign entrepreneurs in Japan. The following is a representative sample:

1. Import of kitchen gadgetry/sports equipment
2. Import of cedar homes
3. Import of upscale French cosmetics, perfumes, and beauty aids
4. Import and export of electronics-manufacturing technology
5. Import of specialty pet foods
6. Preparation of corporate communications materials
7. French restaurant business
8. Shipping company
9. Export of Japanese fabrics
10. Sale of fine Japanese art/antiques
11. Distribution of specialty beer dispensers, aluminum containers, and non-corrosive tubing
12. Personnel placement firm
13. Film distribution and entertainment promotion
14. Computer sales, servicing, and program development
15. Technical advertising and import of orchestral quality oboes
16. Sale of pearls
17. Sale of European art books and arrangement of gallery showings for European artists
18. Fitness center operation and health consultation services
19. Translation services
20. Promotion and import of eucalyptus oil/computers
21. Promotion and import of New Zealand fruit juices and wines
22. Sale and import of New Zealand sheepskin, woolen, and leather items
23. Import and distribution of handbags and accessories

24. General trading company
25. Sale and rental of furniture and interior decoration services
26. Import of French home furnishings and fabrics
27. Architectural, interior design, and space planning services
28. Sale of American baked goods
29. Advertising agency
30. Financial planning services
31. Market entry consulting business
32. Direct marketing services

Foreign businesses in Japan, as can be seen from the above sample, though small in scale, serve both foreign and Japanese concerns and, by allowing the foreigners involved to achieve personal goals, contribute to the flow of trade between Japan and other nations. In line with this position, the Small Business Promotion Committee of the ACCJ prepared a position paper in 1981 which stated that the role of a majority of American small businesses is a cooperative one, assisting large corporations situated in Japan or those based in the U.S. (The same proposition applies to foreign business owners of other nationalities.)

By selling products and/or providing services to domestic corporations, or by offering a representative presence in Japan to overseas businesses, the small businessman serves both the Japan-based community and those outside of Japan as well. Filling the bill on both counts is John McDowell, a "cheerleader" for Barker's Company, a New Zealand producer of fruit juices and wines, who says,"My presence here helps Barker's and does what they can't do—be in Japan."

### SOME SUCCESSFUL SMALL BUSINESSES

André Pachon, restauranteur and owner of Ile de France and Restaurant Pachon in Tokyo, was invited to locate his business in a prestigious building at the invitation of the Japanese owner due to his outstanding culinary talents. He has also been importing French gourmet foodstuffs, which has been of great assistance to other French businesses in Japan.

Dave Wouters runs his own consulting firm and provides a variety of services from personnel placement to insurance underwriting on behalf of AIU, a major insurance company. He has been working in Asia for over 20 years and in Japan for over 17, where he opened his own consulting business in 1976 to focus on employee relations, management consulting, and insurance and business representation. He estimates his revenues for fiscal year 1986 at around $750,000–$1 million (U.S.).

Valerie Gaynard, president and director of Interior Decor and the Interior Boutique, has captured a chunk of the furniture leasing, retail furniture, and interior design market in Tokyo, despite having established her business only two years ago. Currently, she has 18 employees and bills around $2 million in sales.

Dick Adler, president of the Corton Group, manufacturers, importers, and exporters of fiber optics and electronics-related items in Taiwan and Japan, now has over 400 employees, 12 companies, and $30 million a year in revenues. The first Corton company was founded in 1975.

Richard Bliah, French architect and designer, started his business around 10 years ago and now has 3 companies, 18 employees, and an expanding office just recently relocated. His annual billings total ¥300 million.

These small businesses are thus the connecting fibers between larger companies and consumers and between overseas businesses and Japan, a suitable and successful symbiosis.

# 2

# Working with the Japanese

## BASIC BUSINESS PHILOSOPHY

Although it is impossible to do any more than make sweeping generalizations on "how to do business in Japan," I also recognize the need to convey some general information—along with a few words of caution—to foreign men and women involved in setting up or operating businesses in Japan.

### 1. Nervous About Foreigners

Since the Japanese are exactly that, nine times out of ten, proper introductions and entrées are absolute musts. The Japanese want to understand your motivation, personal background, and trustworthiness-rating, so if a mutual aquaintance says you're A-OK, you then become acceptable to your prospective Japanese client, business partner, or contact. The doors will open with the intermediary's aid, so please think of the Japanese "matchmaker" as your golden key. Bluntly, cold calling is taboo.

### 2. The Key Man Is The Key

Opening doors is actually only a part of the process of breaking into the world of Japanese business. If the door opens to reveal a low-level, relatively new employee, or anyone who is not the owner of the business, be prepared for an uphill battle.

In Japan, finding out who is the key person is critical, since businesses are often run by representatives of the owner; that is, the president's office is not always synonymous with the owner's. Ferret out who calls the shots and aim to meet the high guy on the totem pole. The Japanese consensus decision-making process means that it may take time to finally meet the *shachō* (president) or the actual owner, but without the top man at your disposal, business prospects remain poor.

### 3. The Real Thing

"Japanese are not creative; they're copiers." You've heard it a million times, and where there's smoke, there's a conflagration, according to Japanese businessmen willing to admit it. So be creative by offering only the most authentic of products or services. Imitations or outdated goods can be spotted quickly since the Japanese businessman is a sophisticated consumer and a storehouse of information about what's in, what's needed, and what's second best.

Capitalizing on authentic merchandise, such as homemade quilts or granny's cookie recipe, is the way to go as more and more Japanese businesses are clamoring to find specialty goods for discriminating purchasers who study other cultures and lifestyles like no other people do. The Japanese want no disparity between the things they see on holiday trips abroad and what they can buy in Japan.

Imitations or anything in the previous year's mode (unless part of the current "retro" boom), do not impress the savvy Japanese consumer.

### 4. The Presentation

When bringing your product or concept to Japan, a picture-perfect presentation is necessary. For example, because the Japanese will want to know how to adapt for space considerations, a franchiser might demonstrate a restaurant's appearance by using photos, giving details about the size of the original business overseas, and explaining the origins of the enterprise. (Remember that everything costs, at base, several times more in Japan, so supermarket-sized shops and restaurants must be pared down.)

Thus, costs, space limitations, and Japanese nervousness at having to deal with "the foreigner" make it essential that your presentation is superbly detailed down to the last yen, that it presents ways to adapt to the market (especially where space is at issue), and has lots of photos. (Japanese are visual people—remember all of those *kanji,* the thousands of pictographic characters!)

## 5. Impressive Credentials
When meeting with the Japanese for the first, or any, time, "never be late" is the cardinal rule. If you're five minutes late, it paints a bad image, so instead of taxis, use the subway, as this mode of transportation is invariably punctual and reliable. Ten minutes late? You might as well not show, since the unfavorable impression created will taint the atmosphere, said one Japanese manager.

When you do go to the appointment or if you just drop in, be sure that it's never around lunch time, which is usually from noon until one p.m. Stopping in at that time would clearly show that you know nothing about Japanese business practice or are extremely rude and inconsiderate (because you have interfered with the scheduled dining time).

At the first meeting, the *meishi* (business card) is vital. (More on this aspect of Japanese etiquette on page 110.) Never leave home without it, à la your American Express card, or you'll be relegated to the status of persona non grata and may be extremely embarrassed by looking like an orphan—every person needs a company or "parent" or, at the very least, a business title.

Miss Manners would probably approve of my suggesting that you not be too casual at business meetings with your Japanese contacts. Dress up, because appearances *do* count a lot more in Japan, especially when you are the foreigner.

Talking about your background and personal history is a good idea because the Japanese will want to know, being extremely curious about foreigners. Present your curriculum vitae conversationally and emphasize your interest in Japan, its culture, its food, and its people.

### 6. Communication Breakdown

Check your Japanese business contact's English ability if you cannot speak fluent Japanese. If you have any doubts about the ability to be understood or vice versa, you probably need a bilingual go-between.

However, a foreign businessman who can speak Japanese fluently is the best option out of three possible combinations: Japanese translator/foreign businessman, foreign translator/foreign businessman, or foreign businessman who speaks fluently. Why? The ability to speak shows interest in and knowledge of Japan, and helps to avoid misunderstandings.

Brushing up on "a little Japanese" is simply insufficient for real negotiating and nitty-gritty matters, so get it all straight from the beginning by finding a good translator.

### 7. Vague Language

The Japanese language is reputed to be vague and ambiguous, and Japanese businessmen use the language to achieve just that effect on occasion—a handy language, right? For example, *nochihodo* or "later on" should be distilled to exactly when. *Tabun daijōbu deshō* or "maybe, it's ok" should be honed to will you or won't you try it, what kind of response are you intending, or are you just thinking about it? *Kitto* or "surely" is another slippery word that needs decoding.

To avoid problems, do get the when, what, who, and how made clear, but don't push. This is, of course, the hard part. (Everybody said it was going to be difficult!) If you push too much for the particulars, you will no doubt anger the contact and set negotiations back. Being clear, not aggressive, is a distinction the foreigner involved in business in Japan must learn.

The Japanese have developed the practice of *haragei*, or "belly talk." Here is an example. Two businessmen, a buyer and a manufacturer's representative, meet. The representative entertains the buyer the whole evening, flattering and cajoling, playing a co-quettish flunkie and buying his guest an expensive dinner and drinks. No mention is made of business, a dirty word, since it is obvious why the representative wanted to see the buyer: to push his company's goods. Both parties know the bottom line, so there is no need to state the obvious.

Since foreigners, even those perfect in Japanese, are not always used to this kind of situation, talking about the specifics *is* highly recommended. Just don't push and don't try to go native by testing your stomach at *haragei*. The advantage of being foreign is to use your "foreignness," meaning that you can be straightforward and get the answers because the Japanese will expect such behavior.

Remember not to play either role, the ugly American (or other nationality) or the Japanized foreigner, bowing lower, eating more raw fish, and swigging more saké than your Japanese host. Both roles will give you bellyaches.

### 8. The Seal of Approval

One director says "yes." You then think that you've closed the deal. Unfortunately, the numbers game is the way business is played in Japan, because, in order to conclude a deal, one usually needs four to five *inkan* stamps (personal seal impressions) on a contract. There may be two or three directors, a manager, and an owner who must stamp the paper before any jumping for joy is in order, and it usually takes at least two weeks, or sometimes up to a few months depending on the size of the company and how many seals are needed. (Big companies can require as many as 10 seals; small companies need only two or three.)

The waiting-in-the-wings philosophy is, again, applicable here. The pushy, nervous foreigner who wants his *inkan* stamps yesterday may not get them ever. Numerous phone calls to complain about the slow process or one savage tirade about the distracting delay may signal the end of the agreement.

How do you avoid the "*inkan* hell"? One way is to be lucky enough to have a truly unique product that catches the right investor's eye. According to one Japanese businessman, if a Japanese business owner sees merchandise or a concept that is truly special, the business can be started almost immediately. For example, a Kyushu department store president came to Tokyo on a visit and saw some cosmetic items that caught his eye. One month later he opened a boutique that sells the same cosmetic items back home. Evidently, if the product fits the bill, the *inkan* can be edited out.

### 9. Special Feeling

If your product or service is not special or patentable, you should not even try to operate in Japan. While this may be true everywhere, it is an absolute in this market, one of the most competitive in the world.

For example, ethnic clothes, foods, culture, and art, offbeat interiors, gourmet foods, and natural and health products, are all currently in vogue because they are unique and because they can create an impression of individuality for the purchaser.

Why the need for "special feeling," a phrase often associated with Japanese desires? The simplest answer is that while there is a lot of money floating in and out of Japan today, the average Japanese is not wealthy in the Western sense. Since they can't buy bigger houses or more property or an additional car (there just isn't the room), the Japanese often gratify their desires and sedate their frustrations by purchasing goods and, increasingly, services. Thus, price is not a major consideration and may actually lure the buyers if the value-added factors of "special feeling" and "the real thing" are present.

### 10. Fast, Friendly Service and Supply on Demand

A 1950s American gasoline attendant's philosophy is necessary in Japan. That fast, friendly service and supply-on-demand are what Japanese businesses and consumers demand and get. Thus, developing good business relations is not enough if your supplier back home mixes up order specifications or doesn't even come through. (*See* Hugh Kininmonth's comments on page 128.)

Be sure from the outset to provide service on a silver platter, as well as assurances that you can always come up with the goods, even though only time and experience will allay fears that the foreigner can't really be trusted in a pinch. It is the ability to be near perfectionists due to the intensely competitive Japanese market that got the Japanese business set to the top of the heap.

### 11. Golf and *Karaoke,* Anyone?

If you like to tee off or sing sentimental songs (*karaoke*) into a microphone, then participation in these forms of business socializing in Japan will win plus points for you. Business socializing is important to most Japanese businessmen, because it allows them to relax and talk *honne* (one's real feelings), as opposed to *tatemae* (the official line).

While it is difficult for many of the Japanese youth (known as *shinjinrui:* the new breed) to take part in the above activities (and perhaps 10 years from now *karaoke* as a corporate socializing sport may be passé), the fact is that ¥10-million golf club memberships symbolize the continuing status that golf and socializing have in Japanese business. Golf may not fade into the sand pits too soon.

Yet don't imitate Japanese customs or become a *karaoke* fanatic in order to "out-Japanese" the Japanese, as it will be sure to create uneasiness or label you as a strange foreigner. However, if you LIKE joining in the evening drinking and singing binges, and golf games on Sundays are your thing, these activities will break the ice better than anything else.

### TIME IN JAPAN = RETURN ON INVESTMENT

Yes, time does equal money, especially when business is conducted in Japan. There is a direct relationship between the length of residence/interaction with the Japanese and the amount of contacts, knowledge about Japanese ways of doing business, and, it is to be hoped, proficiency in the language. The average number of years in Japan of those surveyed was 12, and most of them had at least 10 years of experience living and doing business in Japan.

The relationship between length of residence and earnings is also apparent. Of those surveyed, tenacity and perseverance had paid off in increased sales and net earnings, since approximately one-half of the entrepreneurs had net earnings of over ¥30 million and had been in business for an average of 15 years.

However, while the general rule is that length of time equals profitability, Witan Associates, a corporate communications firm, has only been in operation since 1982, way below the average time for successful businesses noted above, and yet billed ¥250 million in fiscal 1987. Ms. Bunny Cramer, a managing partner, has been in Japan for 10 years, though, which is certainly a vital factor in Witan's achievements. Ms. Cramer and her partners have between them 35 years of experience living and working in Japan, and it has paid off, as evidenced by the company's billings. "You've got to be prepared to be here and stick it out. This is not a get-in-and-get-out-fast market," she said.

Staying power is of prime importance. Dick Adler of Corton Trading hit upon this phenomena after only three years in business in Japan, when he discovered that he was considered an expert on the Japanese market by overseas customers and on the American market by the Japanese. Early entry and development of personal ties—to gain a reputation as the original "widget" business in Japan—is preventative medicine against latecomer competition.

To graphically demonstrate the principle that Time in Japan = Return on Investment, the following chart shows the number of years in business and the correspondent earnings per year in millions of yen.

**Note:** To obtain the average number of years in business, five categories were established according to net earnings per year in millions of yen. Thereafter, an average was computed for each group based on the number of years in business.

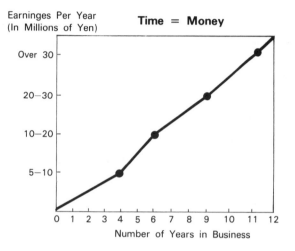

Earninges Per Year
(In Millions of Yen)

**Time = Money**

Number of Years in Business

The results of this study show that "sticking with it" pays off, since length of time in business is directly related to net earnings.

On the average, according to a majority of the people interviewed, it takes five years for a business to show a profit, which is the amount of time it takes to establish credibility, to build contacts, pay off debts, and to carve a niche in the market. The five-year projection is confirmed by the survey results, especially since businesses in the ¥0–5 million category were almost always included in the group of newly established enterprises. As Charlotte Kennedy-Takahashi of Oak Associates remarked, "It takes longer in Japan, about five years, to turn a profit, as opposed to three years in, for example, the U.S., but the rewards are there if you stay at it." Amaury St. Gilles, an art gallery owner with 20 years residency in Japan, concurs. "Start-up time is lengthy, two to three times the normally assumed rate, because you must overcome the language barrier and make yourself known. In Japan, personal relationships are the thing, not the product, and it takes time to make those contacts."

A case history illustrates the principle that investment of time yields income on investment. Reiko Lyster, Chief Executive Officer of Elle International Company, originally came to Japan in 1974 to prop up Revlon's business. She transferred later to Max Factor, which owned Orlane, a prestigious French cosmetics company, and worked on behalf of both companies for four years. She then bought out Max Factor's Orlane interest and established her own company in 1979. Orlane has now become a heavyweight presence in Japan with Ms. Lyster's company doing an estimated ¥1 billion annually in sales.

Ms. Lyster's twenty-year career in a specialized area, the cosmetics business, and subsequent establishment of her own company characterize her as a "classic" foreign entrepreneur. That is, knowledge acquired while working for a larger company was later utilized to set up her own, utilizing the specialty expertise. As Ms. Lyster advised, "Never give up—always be positive. Expect obstacles, barriers, and headaches and be prepared. If you are positive about your own goals and you really try hard, somehow you find a way."

"Don't announce your departure date—it's a security issue," joked Robert White of ARC International, a former Small Business Promotion Committee chairman in the ACCJ (American Chamber of Commerce in Japan). This gets you into trouble when conducting business in Japan, said White, because intent to reside in, work in, and commit yourself to Japan, as well as care for your employees, is of paramount importance. Though resident now in the U.S., White built a company staffed by 125 employees and doing $115 million in business yearly, which put it in the top 5% of consulting companies in the world, all prior to leaving Japan. His eleven-year residency in Japan certainly contributed to that success story.

Ultimately, the most notable point about all the entrepreneurs interviewed, aside from their commitment to Japan and the will to succeed, was the length of time spent in Japan; all told, they had about 400 years of experience in Japan among them, commitment and presence enough.

# 3

# Forming a Company in Japan

## OVERVIEW

Before doing business in Japan, or at some point along the line, the small business must be created legally. Setting up a corporation or deciding to do business as a sole proprietorship must be accomplished, and a capitalization amount, if the former is opted for, must be set aside.

Though not a formally recognized category of business in the Japanese Commercial Code, the sole proprietorship may be chosen, instead of a corporate form of entity. However, liability for business debts rests in full with the proprietor as do all tax obligations, since there is no corporation to ascribe income or liabilities to.

## *YŪGEN-GAISHA* AND *KABUSHIKI KAISHA*

In Japan, there are two types of corporate entities recognized in the Commercial Code, the *yūgen-gaisha* and the *kabushiki kaisha* (abbreviated as Y.K. and K.K.; note that although the correct Japanese term is *kabushiki-gaisha*, the foreign community in Japan has adopted the *kaisha* form). The *yūgen-gaisha* is equivalent to a limited liability corporation, while the *kabushiki kaisha* is a standard corporation, a shareholder-owned, typical stock company.

Due in part to the existence of the title "stock company" and the implied credibility that accompanies that title, the *kabushiki kaisha* form has traditionally been utilized by large corporate ventures and has thus acquired a mantle of prestige and status. Therefore, even small companies have tended to adopt the *kabushiki kaisha* form, although the *yūgen-gaisha* is actually better suited to small business operations, is easier to adopt, and requires less observance of formalities. A comparison of the two forms illustrates this:

| *Yūgen-gaisha* | *Kabushiki Kaisha* |
|---|---|
| *Yūgen shain*, or partner, is the name given to *yūgen-gaisha* contributors to capital, not "shareholders," as in a *kabushiki kaisha*. Units of contribution donated by partners represent units of ownership rather than shares | Contributors called "shareholders"; units of contribution donated by shareholders are termed "shares" |
| "Partners" limited to 50 | Unlimited, since public offerings may be needed |
| Transfer of "shares" to someone not a "partner" needs consent of all "partners" | Cannot limit share transfer unless such a provision is included in Articles of Incorporation |
| "Share certificates" are not evidence of value | "Share certificates" are evidence of value. |
| No authorized capital; just fixed amount of contribution (¥100,000) | Authorized capital |
| Board of directors and representative directors; no need for an auditor | Directors choose one or more representatives from among themselves; must have an auditor |

| | |
|---|---|
| Establishment procedures simpler; time needed is shorter, and no court inspection | If seven or more promoters set up the company (promotive incorporation), court inspection required, but if shares are offered to a non-promoter (subscriptive incorporation), court approval becomes unnecessary. (In the latter case, seven promoters and a single share offering will suffice.) |
| Calling general meeting of "partners" and decision-making process simpler | More complicated procedures and need for a quorum of shareholders |

Thus, it can be seen that the *yūgen-gaisha* is the tailor-made form for small businesses and indeed has been the traditional form for "mom and pop" stores in Japan.

As to capitalization amounts, the *yūgen-gaisha* has no authorized capital amount but there is a fixed amount of ¥100,000, which must be paid in by the contributors. The *kabushiki kaisha*, in contrast, has authorized capital and a minimum capitalization amount of ¥350,000. (In order to avoid court inspection of the "promotive incorporation" process, however, one share can be "publicly offered" to someone who is not a promoter, transforming the process into a "subscriptive incorporation." In that case, the minimum capitalization amount would be ¥400,000.)

One share of stock in a *kabushiki kaisha* must have a minimum value of ¥50,000, regardless of whether it is par or no-par stock.

"Units of contribution" in the *yūgen-gaisha* must be at least ¥1,000 and members of the *yūgen-gaisha* have "shares" "in accordance with the number of units of contribution." (Article 18, *Yūgen-gaisha* Company Law.)

## AN ASIDE ON CAPITALIZATION AMOUNTS

The following chart is a quantification of capitalization amounts of the companies formed by the business people interviewed for this book.

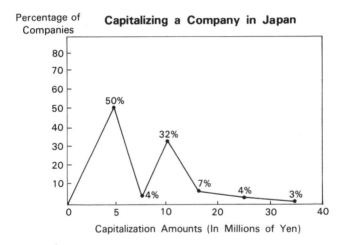

**Note:** In Japan, since capitalization of a company determines the tax bracket for corporate income tax purposes and higher tax brackets expose the company to the scrutiny of a higher ranking tax authority, the large quantity of capitalizations below ¥10 million is indicative of the desire to minimize tax consequences. Also, entertainment deductions are determined by the amount of capitalization, so that companies capitalized at ¥10 million or less are allowed ¥4 million in entertainment expenses, while those capitalized at over ¥10 but not more than ¥50 million are allowed ¥3 million.

The necessity for capital to finance trade, an activity which many small businesses participate in, often causes entrepreneurs to set up new companies rather than increase the capital of an existing company, because higher capitalization is not always a good idea. (*See* Note above.) As Claus Regge of Network, Inc. and Soundwork, Inc. stated, "I formed Soundwork, my second company, because I needed more capital for trade financing and didn't want to increase the capitalization of Network due to tax considerations."

Recently, there have been proposals to provide for a minimum capitalization amount of ¥20 million for a *kabushiki kaisha* and ¥5 million contribution amount for a *yūgen-gaisha*. If such legislation passes, some corporations will have to increase their capital or reorganize within a three- to ten-year transitional period. If companies don't restructure, they will be registered as liquidating corporations by the corporate registry offices, leading to great tax liabilities.

## THE GREAT *YŪGEN-GAISHA* VS. *KABUSHIKI KAISHA* DEBATE

According to the *Yūgen-gaisha* Company Law, Articles 64 and 67, a *kabushiki kaisha* may be transformed into a *yūgen-gaisha* and vice versa, so picking one form does not mean permanent exclusion of the other. In fact, Edmund Daszkiewicz of Procom did change his *yūgen-gaisha* into a *kabushiki kaisha*, upping the capital from ¥3 million to ¥10 million. However, in the opinion of Neil Butler, an Australian who formed his Marumari Company as a *yūgen-gaisha,* when a company's volume of business is small and there is no need for a prestige image, a *kabushiki kaisha* form has no advantages.

As almost 99% of large foreign entities established in Japan are of the *kabushiki kaisha* variety, the use of the *yūgen-gaisha* by small proprietors offers an interesting contrast, which, as several lawyers have noted, is the perfect fit for small businesses. Michael Dunn, a businessman using the *yūgen-gaisha* form, said that since he wanted simplicity, 100% control, and had no partners or investors, the *yūgen* form was the easiest route to incorporation. Since corporate form can be converted readily, as mentioned above, the incorporation of a *yūgen-gaisha* from the outset keeps things simple and is slightly less costly to set up, as will be explained below.

Interestingly, the *yūgen-gaisha* form is more popular among small businesses whose main client base is not composed of Japanese (who regard the *kabushiki kaisha* more highly and view its presence as a sign of permanence). However, it is not necessarily a hindrance to have a *yūgen-gaisha,* even if the clients are mostly Japanese, since many of these types of businesses deal in products that Japanese consumers cannot obtain through other channels. For example, one businessman, an art and book dealer, sells rare and expensive art books imported from Europe that the Japanese cannot locate by themselves. The *yūgen-gaisha* suits his purposes perfectly, he said.

As for running totals, 58% of the people interviewed owned *kabushiki kaisha,* 27% ran *yūgen-gaisha* enterprises, and 15% owned sole proprietorships. The prestige element or lack of knowledge about the *yūgen* form were cited as reasons for using the *kabushiki kaisha,* and besides, many lawyers are simply not as familiar with the *yūgen-gaisha.* Furthermore, good personnel are easier to obtain under the auspices of a *kabushiki kaisha,* a symbol of corporate stability.

## TIME AND COSTS OF SETTING UP

Incorporation can consume time. While manuals on setting up a business state that 30 days are needed to set up a *kabushiki kaisha,* in actuality, it may take much longer if you are doing it yourself. For example, promotive incorporation, as opposed to subscriptive incorporation, takes more time since court inspection is required. Thus, most promoters utilize the subscriptive method of incorporation, using seven acquaintances or law office employees to form the company and then transferring the shares back to the original promoter. However, the necessity of complying with other formalities and a desire for a streamlined procedure lead many small business owners, Japanese and foreign, to conclude that a *yūgen-gaisha* is a better alternative.

One businessman's story will show the problems that may be encountered in setting up a business on your own without professional assistance. According to Walt Spillum of Danco Japan, Ltd., incorporation took a long time due to an absolute penchant for form in the Japanese corporate registration office. The incorporation of Mr. Spillum's two companies took six months and three months respectively, due to the need to be precise and to correct numerical and clerical errors. He concedes that the first incorporation took six months because of an inadequate knowledge of procedures and a lack of funds to pay a lawyer to do it for him. The second company required half the time due to knowledge gained the first time around, but still took three months.

The cost of incorporation is hefty, although it does save time and effort to have a professional do it. The following are the current costs of setting up for both forms:

| *YŪGEN-GAISHA* | *KABUSHIKI KAISHA* |
|---|---|
| 1. Articles of Incorporation: ¥40,000 stamp tax | 1. Same |
| 2. Notary public fee for Articles of Incorporation: ¥41,000–42,000 | 2. Same |
| 3. Attorney's fee: ¥100,000–150,000 | 3. ¥200,000 |

4. Registration fee: ¥60,000 minimum amount. (Calculated by multiplying capitalization amount by 7/1000. If the sum is less than ¥60,000, then ¥60,000 is assigned as the minimum registration fee.)

5. Miscellaneous expenses: certification of authenticity of personal seal or signature (all promoters' seals or signatures); bank's certificate that capital is received; making of personal seal: ¥20,000; ¥5,000 for typing charges; translation fees, etc.

4. Registration fee: ¥150,000

5. Same, excepting making of personal seal: ¥26,000

In relation to Number 5 above, the certification of authenticity of a personal seal (*inkan*) is necessary for all promoters (seven or more for the *kabushiki kaisha* and two or more for the *yūgen-gaisha*), since a seal must be affixed to company statutes and must be certified by a notary public (Commercial Code Article 167). Foreign promoters, due to the difficulty of adducing proof of identification, can substitute a certificate of signature issued by an embassy or consulate of their home countries. However, since a seal is needed to conduct business in Japan, upon obtaining certification of authenticity, have a seal made and register it with your local ward office (*kuyakushō*). Seals cannot be rendered in English or numerals, only the Japanese scripts of *hiragana* or *katakana* or *kanji*. This requirement applies to both *yūgen* and *kabushiki kaisha* forms.

The following information is needed to establish your company, (either form), so have it ready and the process can be speeded up:

1. Name of company rendered in Japanese script or *kanji*, not English or numerals
2. Address of head office
3. Object of the business
4. Certification of authenticity of seals for all promoters or partners
5. Directors and representative directors' names, addresses, and certification of authenticity of seals
6. Auditor's name and address (optional for *yūgen-gaisha*)
7. Shareholders of the *kabushiki kaisha* must list their names, addresses and amount of shares subscribed to, whereas the names, addresses and amount of contribution of two or more partners in the *yūgen-gaisha* must be listed
8. Capitalization amount for the *kabushiki kaisha*
9. Branch name and address of the bank in which capital has been deposited
10. Corporate fiscal year
11. Annual compensation of directors and auditor
12. Intended date of establishment of the company
13. Name and telephone number of contact person in relation to establishment of company

The following documents are also required to set up your *kabushiki kaisha*:

1. Articles of Incorporation that have been notarized
2. Minutes of the meeting of the promoters
3. Minutes of the general meeting of shareholders
4. Minutes of the board of director's meeting
5. Applications of shareholders for subscription to shares
6. Certificate of evidence of paid-in capital and custody thereof by the bank
7. Registration of seal impressions

8. Registration of establishment of the company and power of attorney

An alternative to using a lawyer to register the company, which can easily cost ¥500,000–1,000,000 for consultation and registration, is to employ a judicial scrivener or *shihō shoshi*. The judicial scrivener must pass a test to be qualified and can, for example, register the establishment of corporations, establishment of offices for foreign companies, and increases in capital. Although the sphere of work is confined to registration procedures, the *shihō shoshi* can save the foreign entrepreneur considerable expense if a routine incorporation is desired.

The following is a translation of prescribed charges for *shihō shoshi*, (note the difference in those for attorneys, who can charge ¥15,000–50,000 per HOUR).

| | | **Charge** |
|---|---|---|
| **Establishment of Business**.... | Up to ¥5 million capitalization | ¥21,000 |
| | Up to ¥10 million capitalization | ¥25,000 |
| | Up to ¥50 million capitalization etc.... | ¥30,000 |
| **Increase in Capital** ......... | Up to ¥5 million | ¥12,000 |
| | Up to ¥10 million | ¥16,000 |
| | Up to ¥50 million etc.... | ¥18,000 |

The Tōkyō Shihō Shoshi Kai (Tokyo Judicial Scriveners' Association) has some members that can speak English, but the Association should be contacted in Japanese. Telephone: (03) 353-9191.

An English-speaking judicial scrivener who is highly qualified and recommended is:

Mr. Yasuhiro Abe
5-5-7-517 Toshima
Kita-ku, Tokyo
Tel: (03) 912-2895

Neil Butler, former president of the Australian Business Association, related that after paying ¥200,000 to have his business set up by a company specializing in such matters, he found that he could have saved money by having an acquaintance do it, since the attractive certificate of incorporation did not justify the wasted expense. Perhaps setting up by using a judicial scrivener would save some expenses as well.

Another item that the judicial scrivener can take care of for the small entrepreneur is filings with the Bank of Japan and the Fair Trade Commission; if foreign capital is remitted to Japan to set up the company, these filings must be made as required by the Foreign Exchange Control Law. It is a routine procedure, with BOJ approval taking up to two weeks and mere notification to the FTC being sufficient. Residents (those in Japan more than six months) need not file the reports, unless foreign capital is remitted to Japan to set up the company.

If, however, you are in need of legal advice, an English-speaking, Japanese lawyer who is also a tax accountant is:

Yasumasa Kurokawa
President
Kurokawa International Law Office
Daini Hidaka Building, 4th Floor
3-13-6 Kayabacho
Chuo-ku, Tokyo
Tel: (03) 667-4960

As of this writing, Mr. Kurokawa charges ¥20,000 per hour for consultations with foreign clients. (Expensive, but considerably less than the rates at firms catering to multinational corporations.)

## TRADE NAME REGISTRATION

Under Japanese law, no person can register a trade name that is identical or confusingly similar to one already registered by another, whether a company or an individual, for the same business purposes in the same municipality, town, or village (Commercial Code Article 19). However, this protection is extended only to particularized business purposes, not "general business," for example, and is applicable in only one municipality. Therefore, the business purposes must be specified as in "the widget business and other related business" in order to achieve the broadest protection.

The registration of a trade name does not keep third parties from registering the same name in a totally different area than your retail business, such as wholesaling or manufacturing. Likewise, the protection extends only within the area of the municipality where the trade name is registered. Since Tokyo has 23 wards and there are 652 cities and 2,004 towns throughout the country, you would have to register in every place, which is impossible.

It is usually recommended that a business register its trade name only in the ward where its head office is to be located, since that will give you the right to use your name in the most likely place of use. (Remember, too, that to register the trade name of the company, English and numerical renderings cannot be used, only the Japanese scripts of *hiragana*, *katakana*, or *kanji*.)

Do despair if competitors seize on your name, however, since the Unfair Competition Prevention Law, while prohibiting unfair business practices and allowing the registered owner of a well-known trade name to block the registration of imitators, requires proving intent to misuse and the famousness of the name.

## TRADEMARK AND SERVICE MARK REGISTRATION

The registration of your trademark is an important first step when starting a business in Japan, if dealing in products. The trademark should be applied for as soon as possible prior to commencing business, since Japan, unlike the U.S., for example, has a first-to-register system rather than a first-to-use system. The first to apply has the right to register it, not the first to use the mark.

Your trademark should be distinctive and registration cannot be obtained if the mark:

1. is a common name of the goods;
2. is customarily used with respect to the goods;
3. is a mark that indicates in a customary way the place of origin, sale, quality, raw material, effect, use, quantity, shape, or price of the goods or the method of their manufacture, processing, etc.;
4. is a commonplace family name or title. (This includes, in principle, Romanized names, but is basically confined to names found in the Tokyo metropolis in large numbers.)

The trademark owner can enjoin unauthorized use of identical or confusingly similar marks on articles in the same class, and damages are available. However, in order to become a registered trademark owner, you usually have to wait three to four years, since the workload at the Patent Office is backlogged. If you do get your registration, it lasts for ten years.

Renewal of the trademark can be effected repeatedly, but the mark must be used in relation with the designated goods within three years of the date of application for renewal. (It must be stressed here that use of the mark means use of the trademark as registered, not a variation thereof or use as other than a trademark, for example, as an overall design, since the Patent Office may not consider these valid uses of the mark and not allow renewal.)

As for service businesses that wish to register their service marks, there is, unfortunately, no such registration system in Japan. However, trademarks for goods used in conjunction with the service can be registered. It is hoped that a service mark registration system will be established in Japan in the near future, since these businesses cannot obtain protection for their marks, except under the Unfair Competition Prevention Law.

## THE COSTS/THE SYSTEM

The Japanese legal system is distinct from that of the U.S. in that patent attorneys *(benrishi)*, provide legal advice and effect registration for designs, patents, and trademarks, but are not authorized to deal with other legal areas. The following is a list of current charges for the registration of trademarks that has been established by the Japanese Patent Attorneys' Association. (It applies to Japanese lawyers *[bengoshi]* who provide such services as well.) The "official fee" column is for the charges imposed by the Japanese Patent Office.

| Trademarks | Attorney Fee | Official Fee |
|---|---|---|
| 1. Application for trademark registration | ¥70,000 | ¥14,000 |
| 2. Application for renewal of registered mark | ¥70,000 | ¥14,000 |
| 3. Registration fee for trademark | ¥13,000 | ¥44,000 |
| 4. Search for trademark publication, evidence, etc. | ¥7,000 | |
| 5. Consultation with client (per hour) | ¥28,000 | |
| 6. Translation from English into Japanese | ¥3,400 | |
| 7. Translation from Japanese into English | ¥4,800 | |

**Note:** This is only a partial listing of charges; an official, complete list can be obtained from a patent attorney or lawyer upon request.

Thus, a routine trademark registration, or one without any third party opposition or rejection by the Patent Office, would cost ¥141,000, including application and registration fees.

### JAPANESE PARTNER/GUARANTOR

While many, if not almost all, of the small business entrepreneurs are desirous of going it alone, a Japanese partner/guarantor is an invaluable asset for several reasons.

From the point of setting up the company, unless one is fluent in both written and spoken Japanese, the Japanese partner can, of course, be of great assistance in helping you to understand contracts, obtaining loans, and facilitating relations with Japanese employees. As added plusses, the Japanese partner can provide insights into the culture, and in how to conduct business properly, and can bring a wealth of contacts that provide the entrées so necessary in Japan.

While entrepreneurs do not wish to be beholden to a Japanese partner, often due to mistrust that the Japanese will "steal the business" or because solo spirit balks at such a situation, several entrepreneurs have made happy unions with Japanese and see it as an absolute requirement to entering the market at all. Language problems, bank loans, employee relations, social contacts, and invaluable cultural knowledge are obtained when a Japanese partner enters the picture, according to some of the interviewed.

Chuck Wilson, health and fitness expert and managing partner of Clark Hatch Physical Fitness Centers, particularly emphasized that the Japanese partner was an essential key to success, partly because of the language barrier which may take years to overcome.

# 4

# Financing

## BANKING SERVICES

The first issue in the financing story is that of the role of foreign banks and their lack of cooperation with small business. While one British trader stated that he had relatively little trouble with his U.K. bank due to a long-standing relationship, excepting a high rate of interest, American banks located in Tokyo invariably focus on large companies operating in Japan for practical reasons. Since there is a high ratio of assets managed to staff employed (in large banks, often as much as $1 billion per employee), small businesses are not lucrative enough due to time constraints and priorities. Further, a small rate of return on loans of a larger amount is preferable to a larger amount of return on small-scale loans, according to American bankers. The time involved in making the loans and the lack of availability of trained lending personnel, as opposed to the availability of capital, figures into the policy of the foreign banks operating in Japan. One American entrepreneur noted, "I was eased out by my bank five or six years ago as the lower 50% of their business was dropped as non-lucrative."

As for Japanese banks, since small businesses do not maintain large current accounts, the Japanese bank, far more conservative than its Western counterpart, does not seek out small business customers, whether foreign or Japanese. Very high compensating balances must be maintained, often up to 30% of the principal amount borrowed and outstanding, thus eliminating the majority of small businesses from using the Japanese bank as a financing source. Also, small companies usually like to repay their loans in line with their cash flow cycles, a practice not standard in Japan. Lastly, there is a perception that communciation problems may occur, a perception that persists even if the foreign business owner is quite fluent in Japanese.

## GETTING A BANK LOAN

Background on the three major problem areas provides insight into the dilemma that entrepreneurs in Japan face in relation to financing.

### I. Resident Status

A Small and Medium Enterprise Agency representative noted in l983 that no discrimination existed as to foreign loan applicants applying at government financing institutions, although definite legal questions had existed on whether or not foreign nationals could be financed by the National Finance Corporation (NFC), a governmental organization. Subsequently, due to an order of the Ministry of Finance's Director General of the Banking Bureau, doubts were resolved in favor of allowing financing.

The Small Business Finance Corporation (SBFC), the NFC, and the Japan Develoment Bank make loans without the aid of the Credit Guarantee Association (Nihon Shinyō Hoshō Kyōkai), the public credit supplement system which makes loans without requiring collateral at about a 6% rate of interest and a three-year repayment period—or up to five years if the loan is to be used for operating expenses. And according to the Small and Medium Enterprise Agency, Credit Guarantee Associations located in 47 prefectures in Japan and the SBIC (Small Business Credit Insurance Corporation), which insures the former's guarantees, do not distinguish between foreigners and Japanese nationals. The SBIC is unable to do so, said a representative, since guarantees made by the Association are insured automatically by the SBIC.

It has been stated, however, that some Guarantee Associations have "special standards" for foreigners as an aid to making financial judgments, requiring foreign applicants to have permanent resident status and/or lengthy residency (number of years unknown). The National Federation of Credit Guarantee Associations had, after a speech given by an Agency representative to the ACCJ (American Chamber of Commerce in Japan), been requested by the Ministry of Finance to survey its members' practices more thoroughly, and special standards were ordered to be removed in 1983 by the Board of Governors of the National Federation of Credit Guarantee Associations. However, as one businessman noted, "Standards for granting loans at Credit Associations are variable and seem pulled out of a bag at random."

It was reported in the *ACCJ Journal* that Lyle Fox, an entrepreneur with a bagel business, had applied for a loan through the Credit Guarantee Association in 1984, as his company had been in business for a year, making him eligible. The Association turned him down in spite of the submission of reams of detailed documentation. The reason cited was that he was not a permanent resident, thus contradicting the orders meted out in 1983 by the Ministry of Finance.

The People's Finance Corporation (Kokumin Kin'yū Kōko) told this author that the only requirement as to residence is that the business owner applying for a loan have his business located in Japan and that the guarantor, whether Japanese or foreign, also be resident in the country. No mention was made of "permanent" or "long-term" residence. Since the PFC is a governmental institution, perhaps the official line has been modified, at least for external publication.

## II. The Japanese Guarantor

Small foreign businesses in Japan are not usually able to get a Japanese national to sign on their behalf, which impedes financing efforts, so many of the owners who have Japanese spouses or partners have them sign and assume liability instead, although the former are not always acceptable guarantors if they have no assets or salary of their own. The guarantor problem is a significant one.

Witan Associates' Bunny Cramer received a loan from an American bank that was guaranteed by the Credit Guarantee Association, but only because her Japanese partner signed for it, causing Ms. Cramer and her other partner, another foreign national, to make a separate agreement acknowledging three-way liability. Ms. Cramer also related that a loan with the People's Finance Corporation was guaranteed by her Japanese partner, without whom the loan would probably never have been obtained. "The PFC is very helpful and friendly toward small business, but you probably have to have a Japanese guarantor."

Again, when this author spoke with the PFC, the official line was that the nationality of the guarantor is unimportant; only their financial capability and residence in Japan are scrutinized. The spokesperson also stated that several foreign businesses had foreign guarantors. However, the ACCJ Small Business Promotion Committee and other organizations have had very little luck in opting out of the Japanese guarantor requirement with any governmental institution to date.

In response to the excuse that Japanese nationals are also required to have a guarantor, the contrasting policy of the U.S. Small Business Administration has been that as long as a foreign resident of the U.S. shows that there is a business for which the loan is being applied for, that it is not for an individual's benefit, and that resident alien status is present assuring his/her right to stay in the U.S. and conduct business, there is no nationality requirement or permanent resident status requirement that needs to be satisfied.

To circumvent the Japanese guarantor requirement and permanent resident status problem, Dave Wouters, former Small Business Promotion Committee chairman of the ACCJ, requested membership in 1982 to consider joining the Kyodo Kumiai, an organization affiliated with the National Federation of Small Business Associations. This move, he believed at the time, would strengthen the Committee members' ability to obtain loans through Japanese government agencies and further link the government's resources to foreign small business. A Mr. Hanamura of the National Federation of Small Business Associations spoke to the ACCJ Committee to enlist members, but noted that 50% of a business belonging to the Federation must be owned by Japanese nationals, a requirement that could be arranged through a "paper organization." After becoming a member of the Federation, loans could be obtained by using the Association as guarantor, plus the Association could introduce business partners and consulting services to members. "Many of the problems (of foreign businessmen) come from a lack of communciation," Mr. Hanamura observed.

However, as Wouters explained recently, twenty applications from the Committee were submitted, but "it was a pain in the neck to fill out the forms and go through all of the procedures, so we dropped it. We felt that the red tape was too much." The benefits would have taken extraordinary effort to extract, according to Wouters.

Dick Adler, another former SBPC chairman, has the distinction of being the first foreign business owner to receive a bank loan without a Japanese guarantor's signature. After applying to Mitsui Bank through his Japanese manager for a ¥10 million loan, without collateral, the Credit Guarantee Association guaranteed ¥2 million of the loan without a Japanese guarantor, good for a two-year period. Mitsui provided an additional ¥2 million loan without a guarantee from the Credit Guarantee Association and no signature of a Japanese national was necessary, this part of the loan being a two-month, rollover type. Adler says, "At the time these loans were granted, I was an active member of the ACCJ's Small Business Promotion Committee. Without such backing, I feel that it is highly unlikely that my company would have been granted a loan without either security or the signature of a Japanese national."

## III. Collateral Crunch

Obtaining extension of credit without collateral is next to impossible in Japan for foreign small businesses. As collateral *(tampo)* must consist of cash, deposits in the bank, real property, or stock in a company listed on the first section of the Tokyo Stock Exchange, the extension is not a simple matter.

Furthermore, Japanese banks do not lend money on chattels or finance discount accounts receivable, techniques that are often used in the U.S. Dick Adler of Corton Trading advised, "Exports are the way to go, not imports, because it is impossible to get L/Cs (letters of credit) or credit extended from banks in Japan." Adler detailed the case of a major corporation located in Japan that, despite all its efforts, could not obtain an L/C until two and a half years had passed for credit approval. Small businesses are not even that fortunate.

As stated above, Japanese banks also require borrowers to maintain large compensating balances, up to 30% of the principal, which is next to impossible and at first glance quite contradictory: Why borrow when you already have the money? The People's Finance Corporation has stated in its publicity material that it does not necessarily require real estate as collateral, but the guarantor must, of course, have ample financial wherewithal, a case-by-case analysis being necessary.

### *TEGATA* TROUBLE

The lengthy payment period in Japan is another problem that causes small businesses to seek loans. The payment period for goods in Japan is normally at the end of the month if delivery is effected prior to the 20th of the month. However, if not, the payment time may range widely, sometimes for up to seven months, causing business owners extreme inconvenience and the need to obtain financing for daily business operations. Further, payment is often effected by a promissory note-like instrument called a *tegata*.

*Tegata* issued by banks and companies listed on the Tokyo Stock Exchange may be discounted prior to the date that the note becomes due and owing, usually a period of one to six months after issue. However, due to an 8% charge, the business owner loses money. Notes issued by companies other than these must proceed to maturation first, making the business owner wait to collect payment, and the amount paid does not have its original value due to the time lapse. *Tegata* are a payment method in Japan that small businesses should be aware of, as they are not often equipped to tide themselves over until accounts are paid, contrary to larger concerns with more readily available capital.

Several business owners had encountered a *tegata* problem on a continuing basis, emphasizing the need for cooperation from a bank to finance the business for a period of anywhere from 120 to 150 days in order to cover expenses while waiting for the maturation period to run. However, without the necessary collateral, banks will not extend credit, as stated above.

An importer of pet food talking about the *tegata* system decried, "With payment periods of up to six or seven months, with expenses to meet, how can you run a business?" Since this person had land in Japan suitable for collateral requirements, however, a departure from the norm, he was able to get bank loans, which allowed him to stay in business.

## ALTERNATIVE FINANCING

Some alternatives, direct and indirect, are available for small traders. A newly developed loan program that aids the consumers, rather than the business owner directly, has been formulated by Business Security Pacific K.K., a subsidiary of an American bank. These loans are especially good for foreigners who reside in Japan and cannot get financing to purchase a product, for example, although the interest rate will be higher than Japanese bank loan rates. This type of loan aids customers seeking to buy a cedar home from Walt Spillum's Danco Japan, Ltd., for example, but not to finance the trade operations directly. (Business Security Pacific K.K. may be contacted at (03) 346-8381.)

A second financing method originates with the Tokyo Municipal Government, which contacted Dick Adler of Corton Trading directly to inform him of their policies. The government, along with the Credit Guarantee Association, offers a variety of loans at interest rates ranging from 4.4–6.6%, no collateral required in some cases, for up to ¥70 million and with varying repayment periods. Application may be made with a bank and then the government will check the business's qualifications (businesses must have been in business for more than one year at the same location in Tokyo). The loans are supposedly not tied to product sales, so service sector businesses may qualify. However, the amounts of money available are not clear. One businesswoman noted that Dick Adler was told that ¥30 million is the upper limit, so it no doubt means they intend to loan considerably less.

Thirdly, Guy Cihi, a vice-president of Nippon Fund K.K., has noted that finance companies are a possible "bright side" financing alternative for small businessmen. These companies, such as Dai Shimpan and Orient Finance, are often subsidiaries of banks or credit card companies, and buy accounts receivable or consumer sales accounts, collecting directly on the accounts and charging interest on them, sometimes paying business owners directly within ten days, but reducing the amount paid to cover bad debts.

What about help in the U.S. for American entrepreneurs in Japan? The U.S. Small Business Administration, for example, has never lent to such businesses, as they are permanent establishments in a foreign country, and are thus not considered "American" enterprises. Alternatively, the Foreign Sales Corporation (FSC), created by the Deficit Reduction Act of 1984, came into effect on January 1, 1985, and is designed to require U.S. exporters to sell through a corporation located in a U.S. possession or in a country with an agreement to exchange tax information with the U.S. The legislation was designed to aid U.S. exporters by providing tax exemptions and creating a foreign presence—particularly in developing countries who were complaining about a lack of U.S. investment. While the FSC requires that the exporter perform all manufacturing and production in the U.S., it may indirectly aid the foreign entrepreneur in Japan by allowing its supplier or U.S. exporter to gain tax exemptions and designate the small business as its representative, thus complying with FSC requirements, but direct benefits as to U.S. taxable income for the business owner in Japan are nil.

One other idea that has been bandied about recently at ACCJ Committee meetings is the following. A large overseas client may be able to guarantee a revolving loan at a bank in Japan. This would allow the business to get financing and delete the requirement of a Japanese guarantor, but the overseas client must be willing to put its name on the dotted line and should be a major company. No small business has used this option yet, however.

## SOME CASE HISTORIES

The stories of some small businesses can illustrate the problem of financing a small company in Japan.

Walt Spillum, president of Danco Japan, Ltd., imports cedar home packages for consumer purchase. In need of trade financing, he visited various government institutions and banks but was repeatedly refused. After the third turndown by the National Finance Corporation (NFC) because of claims that the company was too young or had moved within the past year or was too small, Spillum ascertained that his "foreignness" was keeping him from obtaining financing. "I was tainted by being a *gaijin* [a foreigner]," he said.

Ultimately, Spillum did get his financing, although his request for ¥10 million was eventually whittled down to ¥5 million. How did he do it? Specifically, since he was a member of the ACCJ, which has access to Japanese government officials, ACCJ's clout influenced the Small and Medium Enterprise Agency of MITI to give him a loan. Since the Agency regulates the People's Finance Corporation, ACCJ's contact and constant surveillance of the matter at the higher echelon filtered down to lower levels and enabled the loan to be processed without the need for a Japanese guarantor, a requirement Spillum was attempting to delete. His collateral was a house and land valued at ¥21 million, along with his signature. The ¥5 million loan at a 7.9% interest rate and a payment period of four years and seven months was a first: he needed no Japanese guarantor. What had been denied several times was granted in two months with ACCJ's help.

The problem of developing a system of financing that is consistent and reliable remains, as opposed to the current case-by-case basis. Spillum's case appears to have been a specialized one in which ACCJ's muscles and contacts with MITI proved vital, and since Spillum has continued to seek financing since 1984 when the historic loan was granted, the method is not a surefire one. On the bright side, Sanwa Bank subsequently called on him several times to talk about extending a loan after opening an account with that bank, noting that no Japanese guarantor would be needed, only an investigation of company records.

Other Japanese government agencies have been contacted by small business owners such as the Ex-Im Bank, the Small Business Finance Corporation, and the Japan Development Bank, and the atmosphere seems optimistic, although the size of the loans that they traditionally deal in is way too large for small entrepreneurs. (SBFC lends from ¥25 million to ¥200 million and the Japan Development Bank makes loans of over ¥200 million.) However, these larger institutions may be willing to deal with entrepreneurs in the future, some foreign businessmen feel, since the policy of the Japanese government to promote imports to rectify the trade imbalance is being stressed these days.

Favorable reactions have been reported to the idea of some of the above larger institutions lending to small, foreign businesses. For example, Spillum noted that the Japan Development Bank had heretofore reacted negatively to such loan applications, but has indicated its willingness to work with him, although his loan amount of ¥100 million was smaller than the usual amount that the organization finances. Likewise, the Ex-Im Bank has shown an interest in financing possibilities, but postpones commitment until goods complete customs inspection. Spillum says that this requirement is an "NTB," or non-tariff trade barrier, rearing its ugly head, but does believe that the climate is changing and that with different representatives at Ex-Im, perhaps things will change.

(Interestingly, a 1984 application at Ex-Im by Spillum had been unsuccessful as the organization would only finance 70% of the loan with a Japanese bank's cooperation required for the remaining 30%. Since a commercial Japanese bank could not be found to manage that 30%, the loan fell through. However, since Ex-Im had only dealt with ¥200 million loans and over to that date, the fact that it even considered Spillum's application for a ¥50 million loan was amazing.)

Luck is not to be overlooked as playing a role in getting financial backing in Japan. Reiko Lyster, a former SBPC chairman, insisted that it was sheer luck that enabled her to start a business. She met a cooperative, unusually aggressive Japanese banker who took an interest in her proposal to form her own company and initiated the financing process, even matching her up with an investor and financial backer. Without such an active and interested role being assumed by this unconventional Japanese banker, Ms. Lyster stresses, her business would only be an "if" today.

A "tactic" employed by André Pachon, a restauranteur, is instructive. After working for over seven years for another restaurant owner, the Frenchman was offered the business by his employer, who signed as his guarantor at the bank. Establishing a good relationship with an employer and buying him out while using his name on the bank loan are activities that involve time, good personal relations, and fortuitousness.

The final caution on financing may be gleaned from the story of Valerie Gaynard of Interior Decor, Ltd. Ms. Gaynard started a furniture leasing business in 1985 with the investment of $1 million (U.S.) by two Japanese backers. After building a successful venture in a matter of months, she discovered that her benefactors were "members of a Japanese syndicate." After leaving with her righthand executive assistant, Ms. Gaynard started Interior Decor, Ltd. and Interior Boutique. She is determined never to give up, even though she had to deal with a lawsuit brought by the former backers. "It pays to investigate all about who you are doing business with, particularly when it concerns your financing," said Ms. Gaynard.

## FINANCIAL TIPS AND INVESTMENTS

"Your best return on investment in Japan comes from managing your cash flow and *not* trying to make money on the stock market. Figure out your costs, know how to get revenue without spending excessively, and always keep spending to an absolute minimum," said Ms. Debbie Wetmore, managing director of her own company, Wetmore Financial Programs K.K. According to Ms. Wetmore, this market is not a get-rich-quick one, and it is too risky to try to do so due to the currency fluctuations and questionable practices many companies use to pump up demand for their securities.

Ms. Wetmore recommended investing start-up capital in unexciting, but safe, short-term, fixed-time deposits of six-month or one-year increments. These deposits *(teiki yokin)* are tax free, and give the depositor good standing with the bank which can be useful when seeking loans at a later date. (Since Japanese banks only tend to pay attention to those customers with *teiki* or who have outstanding loans, investing in this manner is a good way to get consideration; big savings accounts alone mean nothing to Japanese banks, Ms. Wetmore noted.) *Chūki kokusai* (medium-term government bond funds, usually abbreviated as *chūgoku*) are also recommended for their safe but steady returns.

Ultimately, cash-flow management, or constantly estimating one's costs and adjusting the budget, is a painful necessity and the best "investment" overall. Reworking the estimate is as necessary as making one up, and an accounting firm does not have to be employed to do so. Ms. Wetmore's recommendation, based on personal experience, is not to hire anyone on a retainer basis, such as accountants or lawyers, but to have the job done on an as-needed basis. Furthermore, changing yen amounts to your home currency can graphically illuminate exactly how much money you're spending. "There's a tendency in Japan to think of ¥10,000 as cheaper than it is since everything is more expensive here. So, before you know it, you've spent ¥100,000, and on what?"

Concerning the investment in your business, it was suggested that start-up capital and business financing are not the only considerations, but a long, hard look must be taken at personal lifestyle requirements. The cash-flow burden of starting a business and living in a style to which you are accustomed overseas are real issues that must be tackled, the latter being more important in Japan due to cramped, expensive, and not readily available housing. In other words, there is a limit to one's sacrifice, so if you can't rent and live like a highly paid expatriate employee, investment in business and your personal lifestyle must be carefully calculated, and constantly adjusted to allow for hidden costs, which always creep in. As to hidden costs, Ms. Wetmore recommends the following:

1. Have a checking account at a bank rather than using auto-

matic bank transfers *(genkin furikomi)* to make payments, because the transfer charges run from ¥400–800 each time. "If the creditor doesn't accept my checks, I don't do business with them," she said.

2. To avoid excessive publicity expenses, she suggested making your own advertising, since the proprietor is always the most knowledgeable about the business, not the "experts."

3. Telegraphic transfer rates are expensive and vary constantly from bank to bank and from day to day, it seems, and banks charge commission on money coming in and going out of Japan. Depending on bank promotion efforts, these rates vary so much that a quote must be requested each time a transfer is to be made. "Citibank, for example, wants new customers so they now cost less, but it still varies." Ms. Wetmore was quick to add that when transferring large sums of money, the fees can be negotiated! The solution: always ask.

4. Get quotes from several suppliers of office supplies or equipment and then *negotiate*. The Japanese do bargain, contrary to popular belief, and prices change so often, even within the same supplier's business, that you must ask each time you want to make a purchase. Ms. Wetmore detailed how an office supplier's prices went up substantially and that she wasn't informed about the increase. "It's a tedious process but they'll nickel and dime you if you don't ask every time."

The best way to keep tabs on all of these petty cost-balancing factors is to have someone in charge of these worries who sees to it that the expenses are kept within the budget. Constant review and supervision are much more important in Japan where the yen seem to flow out faster due to high overhead.

**The Mature Business.** What about successful, established, and mature small businesses that want to invest excess cash but don't know what to do? Ms. Wetmore suggested purchasing real estate to be considered as both living and business space. Since this form of investment is yen-based, no currency risk is present and the ever-climbing land values make it a good plan for business and personal reasons.

As to stock markets, a cautious approach is recommended, even for those businessmen with money to set aside for three or more years. Managed funds and offshore market funds, the latter having the best performance record in the Japanese market, are great for building a diversified equity portfolio, but "caveat emptor" is applicable. This is because Japanese companies have been known to start "bargain sales" of stock to pump demand, and it is also difficult to get real information on the companies. "When you consider investing, the rules of the game are different here. Find out the motivation of the person selling to you. Remember, too, that there is generally less interest in small business investors in Japan."

**Borrowing Issue.** Since banks do not lend money to small businesses, as explained above, keeping close tabs on your currency exposure is a good idea when remitting capital from abroad. After being established in business for a couple of years or so, converting non-yen debt to yen debt is advisable, and the Japanese banks may let you do it, even if the traditional requirements outlined above (resident status, collateral, longstanding relationship with the bank, etc.) are not met.

# 5

# Taxation

## TAXATION OF EARNED INCOME IN JAPAN

**Permanent and Nonpermanent Resident Status.**   Foreign citizens are classified as either permanent or nonpermanent residents for income tax purposes. The distinction is important since the former must pay tax on all income worldwide, whereas the latter are liable only for income tax on income obtained in or remitted to Japan.

If a foreign citizen resides in Japan for more than five years or intends to remain permanently in Japan, even if he or she has lived in the country for less than five years, the classification of "permanent resident" applies. Therefore, a foreign small-business owner could be regarded as a permanent resident, although not in Japan for five years, since the establishment of a business certainly demonstrates the intention to remain permanently.

**National Income Tax for Individuals.**   Every resident, foreign or Japanese, must pay national income tax as well as prefectural and municipal inhabitant's taxes. (Income includes wages, interest, dividends, earnings from a business, etc.) Individuals are obliged to participate in the withholding tax scheme when income from interest, dividends, or salary is paid in Japan, and so are proprietors of businesses (whether a professional or retailer/wholesaler).

Individual income tax rates now range from 10.5–60% effective from fiscal year 1987 due to recent revisionist tax laws passed by the national legislature. Individuals can take a basic personal deduction of ¥330,000 on their national income tax forms and get deductions for dependents, contributions to charities, life insurance premiums, pension premiums, and some medical expenses.

Business income is attributable to a proprietor when there is no corporate form of business, although a taxpayer filing a "blue return," or detailed form to encourage honest self-assessment, may be treated as if his business had been operating as a corporation for the years 1974–88. (Remember that sole proprietors are not allowed to have limited liability.) It should be stressed at this point that a salary received by the owner of a business must be "reasonable," and when it is considered "excessive" by the authorities, the excess is taxed at the rate of 30% or 42% for the excess over ¥8 million. (*See* below.)

## CORPORATE INCOME TAX

If you have a company, after deducting your salary, the remaining income is treated as the corporation's income, which is subject to corporation tax and inhabitant's tax, both prefectural and municipal. Tax rates for a small company (capitalized at less than ¥100 million) are:

| | |
|---|---|
| ordinary income of ¥8 million or less | 30% |
| over ¥8 million | 42% |
| When dividends are paid: | |
| ordinary income of ¥8 million or less | 24% |
| over ¥8 million | 32% |

A closed corporation (50% of its capital owned by one to three shareholders), and persons or companies related thereto, is subject to stricter scrutiny than other types of companies, since tax officers can authorize taxation of retained earnings if the company makes a profit and does not pay dividends. Transactions between family corporations or between such companies and their shareholders resulting in overly low tax burdens can also be denied as these may not always have been "at arm's length," or properly effected.

## INHABITANT'S TAX

Individuals and corporations are both liable for municipal and prefectural inhabitant's taxes. Individuals must pay inhabitant's tax if resident in a prefecture and municipality on January 1 of the year following the year in which income was earned. A corporation having a principal place of business in Japan must pay corporation inhabitant's tax.

Prefectural inhabitant's tax rates for individuals are set at 2% for those with a total taxable income of not over ¥1.5 million, or at 4% for those whose income is over ¥1.5 million. Deductions for prefectural inhabitant's tax purposes differ from those for income tax purposes. Municipal inhabitant's tax rates for individuals vary from 2.5–14% and are levied on total taxable income. Municipal inhabitant's taxes for corporations are calculated with standard per capita rates or a standard tax rate based on income (usually 12.3%). Individuals can take a basic ¥260,000 deduction against their inhabitant's tax.

## ENTERPRISE TAX

This tax applies to both corporations and sole proprietors, and is based on income derived during the previous calendar year (it is levied in the fiscal year beginning April 1 for individual taxpayers). After a proprietor takes his fixed deduction of ¥2,200,000, no other deductions or exemptions being allowed, the enterprise tax is assessed at the rate of 3–5% in relation to the profits of the year before. Payment is usually made in two installments during August and November.

Enterprise tax for corporations, on the other hand, is based on business income and income upon liquidization. Their tax is computed in the same manner as national corporation tax. The standard tax rates for ordinary taxable income are:

6% for income of ¥3.5 million or less

9% for income over ¥3.5 but not above ¥7 million
12% for income above ¥7 million

## MISCELLANEOUS CONSIDERATIONS

Carry-overs for losses are allowed for three years on corporation taxes, but a "blue form" must be filed which requires submitting detailed information on the company to qualify for the carry-over period.

Entertainment expenses may be deducted in larger quantity when a company is capitalized at lower sums. (*See* note on page 37.)

In 1984, an expense account posting system was established by law, and calculation of actual amounts expended, as opposed to estimates, has become the rule rather than the exception. (While no penalties will be incurred if such posting entries are not submitted with your returns to substantiate expenses, expenses that cannot be substantiated are usually non-deductable.) Furthermore, even if a statement of expenses and revenues is not attached, an annual return must be filed by the individual with business income.

"General expenses" include the following: imposts and duties; packing and transportation costs; utilities; travel and commuting expenses; charges for fax, phone, telex, etc.; publicity/advertising costs; entertainment expenses; indemnity insurance premiums; repair fees; supplies; public welfare system premiums. "Special expenses" include salaries and wages; wages for subcontractors; depreciation; bad debts; costs of leasing real estate and business premises; and interest charges.

Both corporations and individuals may take a basic deducation of ¥330,000 against their income tax.

## TAX ISSUES FOR AMERICAN ENTERPRISES IN JAPAN

The Small Business Promotion Committee (SBPC) of the American Chamber of Commerce in Japan formulated a position paper in 1981 decrying the taxation of Americans overseas stating, "No other major country taxes its nationals' foreign-earned income, and the U.S. is certainly not in the financial position to add this disincentive to American investment abroad." The ACCJ's stance on taxation of Americans overseas is that the ability of American employees and business owners to compete is severely hampered by imposition of U.S. tax obligations on them, as a portion of their income is "often subject to double taxation." Thus, the ACCJ maintains that full exclusion of foreign-earned income will only strengthen competitive efforts.

Dealing with both Japanese and U.S. tax rules is costly and burdensome, since the services of an accountant to complete both sets of tax filings are required, a cost that larger businesses can afford but small businesses are hard-pressed to cope with. Aside from accounting costs, the small business has overhead expenses that are deductible but must be paid out of the business owner's pocket, along with two sets of taxes, so one wonders how American small business owners in Japan can make any profits.

A 1981 resolution of the Asia-Pacific Council of American Chambers of Commerce stated that U.S. government programs do not pay attention to American entrepreneurs abroad, but instead focus on large companies. The exclusion of foreign-earned income could be one definite way of encouraging entrepreneurship overseas and helping exports directly, since small businesses are often the link between American exporters and foreign markets.

In addition to the protest against the taxation of foreign-earned income, the ACCJ is strongly urging Congress to repeal the portions of the Tax Reform Act of 1986 that limit the foreign tax credit to 90% of the Alternative Minimum Tax. The ACCJ feels that by limiting the taxpayer's ability to offset tax liability by foreign tax credits, double payment of tax occurs, which is contrary to U.S. tax principles. Double taxation is further reducing American competitiveness, according to the ACCJ.

## A NOTE ON ACCOUNTANTS

Charges for accounting and auditing to ensure proper payment of both Japanese and U.S. taxes, in the case of U.S. entrepreneurs, must not be overlooked when budget planning time appears. A simple bookkeeping, payroll, and tax service for a small office can range from ¥500,000–1 million for one year, depending on the complexity of the services rendered. The high cost of accounting services is due in part to the need for translations from English into Japanese for the Japanese tax authorities. (Detailed reports in specialized Japanese demand that accounting be handled by professionals trained in proper translation techniques. Thus, the costs of accounting for small businesses can easily pile up.)

For example, Debbie Wetmore of Wetmore Financial Programs K.K. was told on her first inquiry about accounting costs that it would be ¥150,000–300,000 for a routine preparation of Japanese taxes. Her second inquiry revealed a reduced sum of ¥80,000, but she felt it was still too high. Finally, she ended up doing it herself, being aided indirectly by the English-language service provided by the local ward office. While the tax service is provided to foreign individuals, not to companies, she did obtain some handy pointers that could be applied to her business.

An accounting firm in Tokyo that is itself a small, entrepreneurial venture is Royce & Taylor. The firm handles mostly U.S. tax returns, but can provide Japanese tax-related services as well for both individuals and corporations.

Mr. Steve Royce
Royce & Taylor
Ishizaka Building # 2-202
1-28-14 Kamitakaido
Suginami-ku, Tokyo 168
Tel: (Toll free in the Kanto area) 0120-26-6441
Fax: (044) 932-7863

For Japanese speakers, the following accountant proved extremely helpful to this author:

Mr. Kazushige Konno
Tobu Godo Kaikei Office
4-11-5 Kotobashi
Sumida-ku, Tokyo 130
Tel: (03) 631-6610

# 6
# Visas

## YOUR ENTRANCE VISA/ALIEN REGISTRATION

In order to enter Japan, a foreign national must possess:
1. A valid passport or "travel document" issued by a Japanese embassy or consulate abroad when a passport cannot be issued.
2. A valid visa stamped in the passport by a Japanese embassy or consulate abroad. (Since visa exemption agreements made between Japan and other countries do not apply to those foreign nationals intending to engage in activity for remuneration in Japan, a visa is necessary.)

However, visa agreements do apply when coming to Japan to participate in business meetings, inspection tours, or just to research information for business purposes. For example, a U.K., Swiss, Irish, Austrian, or West German national can come to Japan for six months or less for those purposes; a French, Italian, Spanish, Swedish, or Dutch national, for three months or less; a New Zealander, for 30 days or less. (Japan has visa exemption agreements with 48 countries, so this list is not exhaustive.)

Lastly, the purpose of entry must be within the scope of the status of residence, which will be detailed below.

**Entrance and Admissions.** "Basically, those who are engaged in trade or management of a business will be admitted [to Japan]," stated Susumu Yamagami, Assistant Director of the General Affairs Division of the Immigration Bureau, at a November 1986 seminar on immigration practices in Tokyo. However, "those engaged in trade must be employed by an enterprise that handles a substantial amount of trade with or investment in Japan," according to Justice Ministry guidelines.

The Tokyo Regional Immigration Bureau recently told a foreign lawyer that a minimum of ¥30 million in capitalization and ¥100 million in revenues were the magic numbers for entrepreneurs trying to employ themselves for visa purposes. Obviously, small businesses cannot meet those criteria at their inception, nor can many medium-sized enterprises, so entry on a "posting visa" for an aspiring entrepreneur is next to impossible.

**Alien Registration.**　　The entrance visa is not, however, the only legal requirement for foreign nationals intending to reside in Japan. Within 90 days of entry, the foreign national must register at the ward office with jurisdiction over the area in which he will live. The "alien registration," as the process is called, requires fingerprinting of the left index finger in a booklet, soon to be made into an identification card, with particulars about the individual and a photograph. It must be carried at all times while in Japan and presented to the police or authorities upon request.

The alien registration application includes name, date of birth, sex, nationality, occupation, passport number, status of residence (type of visa), period of authorized stay, address, and name and location of office where engaged. Any change in these items must be conveyed to the ward office. In particular, notification of renewal of one's visa or change in type of visa must be done, since foreign nationals who forget to do so can be brought in for questioning by the police. Changes in the name, nationality, occupation, status of residence, period of stay, address, or name and location of office where employed must be made within fourteen days of the change. If the change involves moving to another address, the notification must be made at the new ward office.

## STATUS OF RESIDENCE AND PERIOD OF STAY

When foreign nationals enter Japan, the status of residence is determined by the Immigration inspector at the port of entry. "Status of residence" denotes what activities a foreign national is permitted to engage in while residing in Japan. The following is a list of the relevant categories:

| | | |
|---|---|---|
| 4-1-4 "Tourist visa" | Temporary visitors, including those on inspection tours and participants in meetings, courses, and other similar events | 30 days<br>60 days<br>90 days<br>150 days |
| 4-1-5 "Posting visa" | Persons engaged in business management, foreign trade, or capital investment activities | 3 years<br>1 year<br>6 or 3 months |
| 4-1-l6-1 | Spouses or children of Japanese nationals residing in Japan as family members | 3 years<br>1 year<br>6 or 3 months |
| 4-1-16-3 | Persons not falling into any other category but permitted to reside by discretion of Justice Ministry (includes teachers, Japanese-language students) | Up to 3 years, decided on a case-by-case basis |

Period of stay is determined with the status of residence at the port of entry. The duration of the period of stay is determined by the type of status of residence and is calculated from the day following the date of permission. (More detailed information on status of residence can be obtained from the Central Immigration Office, Tel: (03) 580-4111.)

## The Posting Visa Story

While the 4-1-5 posting visa is the classification sought by those engaged in management of a business, foreign trade, or capital investment activities, a 4-1-4 short-term stay visa can be used to enter Japan and obtain information on the market or actually set up a branch or subsidiary of a company. (The 4-1-4 "tourist visas," while primarily for sightseeing purposes, preclude the holder from participating in profit-making activities, but may be used to enter the country to establish a business, a non-profit act.)

When someone comes to Japan as an employee of a subsidiary or joint venture, obtaining a posting visa is not generally a problem. The applicant must show that the business employing him in Japan is viable and stable, as an Immigration officer has characterized the requirements, writing about the reasons for coming to Japan to do business; submitting materials explaining the employment contract terms; having a letter of guarantee written by an individual or corporate guarantor assuming responsibility for the applicant's ordinary expenses, return transportation, and maintenance and support while in Japan; providing a list of the foreign employees at the employer's business and including materials explaining the scale of the business and business records, such as profit and loss statement, tax receipts, and corporate registration; and giving the applicant's personal history. (However, when the business is a fledgling subsidiary, the concern is that the viability and stability requirements may not be met at times, so information on the parent company overseas is often necessary.)

On the other hand, a small, entrepreneurial business established in Japan that is not a branch or subsidiary operation can be the employer and "sponsor" the business owner, but problems have invariably arisen since these types of businesses often cannot show "viability and stability." The Australian Business Association has a member monitoring this visa problem. The Australian entrepreneurs, primarily young people who have decided to remain in Japan after coming to work on a temporary exchange program called "the working holiday plan," want to have their own businesses employ and sponsor them for a posting visa rather than have a Japanese customer provide the documentation and letter of guarantee required by the authorities. Because an obligation arises to perform strictly for that customer and the prospect of asking a customer or client to "employ" the small business owner solely for visa purposes is unsavory, independent-minded entrepreneurs are certainly reluctant to go that route.

It seems that after a track record is established and financial viability can be proven and is assured, a business owner may have his own company employ him and provide sponsorship to obtain the coveted posting visa. The viability and stability requirements are to ensure that the foreign entrepreneur does not become a burden on the Japanese welfare system by requiring unemployment assistance, and that the business owner has created jobs for Japanese nationals in accordance with the Justice Ministry's policy of regulating immigrants so that full employment of Japanese can be fostered.

Quite a few of the business people interviewed expressed frustration about the posting visa dilemma in regard to self-employment. One Australian noted that as long as one has *permanent* residence status there is no problem with self-employment for posting visa purposes. Another entrepreneur felt that since the Japanese immigration authorities looked askance at his visa application, which listed his business as a sole proprietorship, it was necessary to get sponsorship from a language school where he could teach part-time. Valerie Gaynard of Interior Decor, Ltd. had only a two-year track record in Japan, but since she employed 14 Japanese and had $2 million in revenues, she suspects that the Immigration people were forced to give her a posting visa, although it was necessary to have a member of the Diet (Congress) make some timely telephone calls on her behalf. Several other people said that although a posting visa took a long time to obtain, it was only good for a one-year period of stay, making business planning extremely difficult and the uncertainty of renewal an ever-present headache.

The Australian Business Association has formulated a position paper on this critical problem, of which the following is an extract:

> The heart of the problem is that current Japanese immigration regulations and the way they are administered do not appear to allow a small foreign businessperson to operate independently in Japan in a commercially sensible and stable fashion. There is no category of visa which specifically allows for small business people to enter Japan and operate here on a realistic basis. The Japanese 4-1-16-3 (see above for details) appears to be a very flexible visa, and immigration officials have stated in the presence of ABA members that there is provision for independent entrepreneurs to sponsor themselves. However, in practice the guidelines appear to be totally unrealistic, and the two ABA members who are known to have applied for self-sponsorship were refused. The situation is further complicated by the fact that the Japanese immigration authorities publish little information on their immigration procedures and how foreigners should proceed in order to comply with their law. There is widespread confusion among members as to what the situation really is, and we have now amassed enough evidence to be able to state categorically that different members have been given contradictory information by different Japanese officials. This situation has led some individuals to start businesses in the belief that they could do so, only to run afoul of the Japanese immigration authorities to their considerable disadvantage. . . .
>
> There are two principal handicaps. One is that the situation is too unstable to allow a small business to plan for the long term, and to enter into long-term contractual arrangements with Jap-

anese partners, and also employees. The second problem is that small businesses may lose the investment return on any money they bring into the country. . . .

Ideally, we would like written guidelines from the Japanese government as to what their regulations really are. . . . Otherwise, . . . there are two likely avenues to follow in seeking a solution to our problems. . . . The Japanese 4-1-16-3 visa seems very flexible, and it appears that if the Japanese wanted to, they could probably . . . relax the critera they appear to apply to people seeking self-sponsorship as independent entrepreneurs. Commercial realities require that the term of the visa granted would have to be longer than the one year normally granted under this status. . . .

Alternatively, it may be possible to set up some small business exchange program on the model of the working holiday scheme.

At a recent ABA meeting, it was noted that members did not know how to make applications because "it is believed that there may be a whole superstructure of regulations and procedures . . . that the authorities will not make public." Because members did not know what was expected of them, they could not make effective applications. Thus, when an Immigration advisory official states that ¥30 million in capitalization and ¥100 million in revenues are the requirements for self-sponsorship, but other small business owners not meeting these criteria apply for and get visas, the ABA's discovery of the discrepancy in advice offered by Justice Ministry officials is underscored.

As for bottom-line considerations, according to a great number of the entrepreneurs interviewed (not just the Australians), investing for the long term is made difficult when visa troubles are present. Further, the Japanese system of requiring foreigners to have personal guarantors and corporate sponsors as well for employment purposes puts entrepreneurs in a precarious position, and not a few have been exploited by Japanese companies due to their unequal bargaining position. Since almost all entrepreneurs have an interest in Japan, have studied Japanese, etc., the obstacle to admission of foreign small business owners to the Japanese market is, as ABA has stated, "difficult to comprehend."

The following documents are required to be submitted when applying for a posting visa. (Keep in mind that self-employment for visa purposes is extremely difficult and the actual documentation and information needed to show stability and viability, the official criteria, are not clearly delineated.)

### Posting Visa Documents

(These are general guidelines only. Please consult with Immigration before undertaking application procedures.)

1. Reasons for coming to Japan to do business
2. Particulars on foreign employees
3. List of all employees
4. Materials explaining scale of the business and business records, including tax receipts, corporate registration, profit and loss statement
5. Applicant's personal history
6. Guarantee issued by a guarantor living in Japan assuming responsibility for applicant's ordinary expenses, return transportation, maintenance and support while in Japan
7. Business plan, including prospective amount of sales for the future year
8. Materials showing trade business accomplishments

**The 4-1-16-1 Visa.**　One possible way out of the problem of visa sponsorship is, as a foreign lawyer has jokingly noted, marriage with a Japanese national. A 4-1-16-1 family visa can then be obtained, which allows the holder to work without restrictions, excepting at illegal employment, and to change jobs without notifying the authorities, which must be done for other visa classifications. This visa is granted for a term of three or six months, one year or three years, but applicants are not usually granted a three-year family visa right away. Comparatively speaking, however, the family visa seems to be granted with fewer restrictions in Japan than in the U.S. due to recent reforms in the U.S. Immigration Control Act.

**The 4-1-16-3 Visa.**   While this category has been created for those professions that do not fit neatly into other categories and is a flexible denomination, the 4-1-16-3 visa is not yet able to be used by foreign entrepreneurs, although the ABA would like to see that category utilized for self-sponsorship.

## PERMISSION TO ENGAGE IN ACTIVITIES OTHER THAN THOSE PERMITTED UNDER STATUS OF RESIDENCE

Foreign nationals resident in Japan can only engage in activities falling under the status of residence. If the person wants to participate in other temporary or secondary activities that are not subsumed by the present status of residence, permission must be applied for in advance.

If the permission is not applied for, Article 24, item 4 of the Immigration Control Act mandates deportation of the foreign resident who engages solely in activities other than those permitted by the present status of residence. Engaging in some activities not permitted by the present status of residence subjects the foreign resident to the likelihood of non-renewal of the visa, a possible fine of up to ¥200,000, and up to six months penal servitude (Article 73 of the Immigration Control Act). Also, anyone knowingly employing such a person can be charged as an accomplice.

Two copies of the application form requesting permission to

engage in other activities, one copy of any materials indicating in definite terms the type of activity to be engaged in (i.e., copy of employment contract, information about the business of the employer, etc.), and one copy of a certificate describing the present activities engaged in are all required. (Officials can, however, request more than one copy of the various documents.)

The above requirements and the needs of aspiring, foreign business owners in Japan do not dovetail, however. Since aspirants employed by other institutions in Japan who are not married to Japanese nationals often cannot show "viability and stability," as explained above, they often try to get a toehold in the market while continuing in their present position, seemingly the most obvious and safe way to go about setting up your own business.

However, since applying for permission to engage in other activities is like waving a red flag at the Immigration authorities, and of course, causes problems with the current employer, the application process is not a helpful way to get your business in shape, although it is legally required for those trying to strike out into other areas. Cases of subterfuge are, unfortunately, not uncommon (for example, an English teacher employed at a language school who decides to start working toward establishing his own). The law and the reality of the marketplace are at odds, according to many of the business people interviewed.

## PERMISSION TO CHANGE STATUS OF RESIDENCE

When a foreign national decides to switch to a new activity falling outside the present status of residence, he should apply for and obtain a change of status of residence. These applications are not automatically approved, however. (Notably, 4-1-4 temporary visa holders usually cannot have their status changed to another within Japan.)

If someone participates in activities solely outside the scope of the permitted status of residence without getting permission first, he is subject to deportation and/or up to three years penal servitude and up to ¥300,000 in fines (Article 70, Immigration Control Act).

Documents to be submitted when changing the status of residence include:

1. Two copies of the application for change of status of residence
2. One copy of the statement of reason for making an application to participate in a new activity
3. One copy of materials concretely stating the nature of the new activity
4. Letter of guarantee by a guarantor resident in Japan, either foreign or Japanese, with financial capability sufficient to ensure maintenance of applicant while resident in Japan, return transportation, and ordinary expenses
5. One copy of materials certifying guarantor's financial capability (i.e., certificate of tax payment or employment)

Applicant may be requested to submit two copies of each document by Immigration officials, so be prepared.

## IMMIGRATION OFFICES

The following are a few of the main immigration offices in Japan:

1. Tokyo Regional Immigration Bureau
   1-3-1 Otemachi, Chiyoda-ku
   Tel: (03) 213-8111
   (This office has jurisdiction over Tokyo, Kanagawa, Niigata, Saitama, Gunma, Chiba, Ibaragi, Tochigi, Yamanashi, and Nagano prefectures)
2. Yokohama District Immigration Office
   37-9 Yamashita-cho, Naka-ku
   Tel: (045) 681-6801
   (Jurisdiction over Kanagawa Prefecture)

3. Osaka Regional Immigration Bureau
   2-31 Tani-machi, Higashi-ku
   Tel: (06) 941-0771
   (Jurisdiction over Osaka, Kyoto, Hyogo, Nara, Shiga, and
   Wakayama prefectures)
4. The Central Immigration Office
   Immigration Bureau, Ministry of Justice,
   1-1-1 Kasumigaseki, Chiyoda-ku, Tokyo
   Tel: (03) 580-4111

# 7

# Employees

## IN GENERAL

As of this writing there are 409 employees working for the business people interviewed for this book, evidence that the small foreign business uses a lot of manpower. The difficulty, however, is obtaining quality people and then keeping them, because the two strikes against the small foreign business, its size and its foreignness, make it unattractive to most corporation-bound college graduates.

Because the small foreign company is competing with big business for good employees, all of the benefits offered by the former must be in line with those of the latter, an expensive and usually impossible thing to do. Chuck Wilson, managing partner of Clark Hatch Physical Fitness Centers, stated, "Japanese don't usually want to work for a Western company because they want to be associated with Japanese institutions due to the contacts and image."

Other entrepreneurs stressed that is virtually impossible for a small foreign company to hire Japanese staff, not because of the less attractive benefits, but because of the lack of security and seeming instability these types of businesses present. Thus, psychological and financial needs are both equally important considerations for the Japanese employee.

## EMPLOYEE ALTERNATIVES

Men and women operating businesses in Japan repeatedly stated that because of the character of the business, they encountered "the classic problem" of finding good personnel. As one man said,

"When I started out, it was so difficult because no young Japanese wanted to sign on; they wanted to work for a big Japanese company. As my company grew, though, I used housewives and retired men and have done very well with them." This particular person now boasts 40 regular employees plus a sub-agent distribution system employing 80 people throughout Japan by using "employee alternatives"—housewives and retired men.

The secret to hiring good employees lies in the foreign entrepreneur's ability to choose from those Japanese that have an ability to fit in with the small foreign business, or by using women, the retired, and the social "nonconformist" type. These are often people looking for value-added employment or something that isn't available at larger, more bureaucratic outfits, including: a chance for rapid advancement; specialized training; a titled position (which takes years to achieve at a larger company); shorter working hours; and more challenge and responsibility in general. Direct benefits which are received sooner in a small company, and are tied to individual performance, are attractive to the housewife looking for challenges, to retirees who would like to use their skills, and to nonconformists who do not readily fit into large companies.

The profile of the social nonconformist is usually that of a Japanese who has had overseas experience, either working or going to school, or who lacks a prestigious educational record. These people often want to escape "the system," and tend to be more flexible than the average Japanese salaryman who is a product of Japan's rigid school system. As an example, one Japanese business manager of an entrepreneurial business lived in California for a few years as a "hippie," and he later decided to work for a small foreign company for the three usual reasons: he liked his boss's personality and style; he did not want to work for a traditional, life-time employment type of company with all of the attendant bureaucracy; and he believed that the product was a quality one and felt positive about introducing it to the Japanese market.

Some entrepreneurs felt that Japanese society was changing and that capitalizing on the changes in young people was also another "alternative." For example, the Montrive Company, run by Israeli Aron Meron, imports bags and accessories and has about 60 young employees throughout Japan. "Good income and a good position are increasingly important to the young Japanese," said Mr. Meron, who has lured the young generation with these benefits.

Of course, some business owners have opted out of the Japanese system, so to speak, and are using only foreign personnel for their operations, or very few Japanese employees. One woman gave commissions to unemployed, expatriate housewives and avoided hiring too many Japanese, except as clerical, part-time workers. Since most of her business is concentrated on the foreign community, this was a viable option.

### KEEPING JAPANESE EMPLOYEES

André Pachon, restauranteur, has said that the problem isn't finding good employees, as many Japanese want to learn the way of French cuisine, it's keeping them. "They don't stay long—maybe two or three years at most." An American, formerly running a home-baking business, also had such a maintenance problem that she found herself in the kitchen baking, rather than doing the necessary promotional work on the outside, because she had trouble keeping a steady core staff. "You need people that won't suddenly quit. You can't find a good person to stay on in charge of operations. I guess what I need is a thirty-year-old divorcée who wants good money if she works hard."

Without examining potential employees for "fitness with the enterprise," many mistakes are made, Edmund Daszkiewicz of Procom noted. "Quick finds breed mistakes. We now take a medium- and long-term view and target people for stability and the medium term, not just urgent needs." He joked that it is obvious when someone does not fit into the business, recalling that one man left after only three days.

Jane Yonamine of Yonamine Pearls detailed her employee prerequisites after over 20 years' experience in business in Japan, speaking highly of her manager of over fourteen years who was trained in the U.S. to understand how to work with American clientele. Ms. Yonamine said that she offers a higher base pay than a Japanese company would in order to portray an aura of security and to attract good people. While she still pays salaries in the Japanese manner (monthly salary, plus biannual bonuses), she bases raises on productivity, not seniority, and pays "generous overtime." Lastly, she stressed that English ability is certainly not the only important skill, although many foreign businesses, both small and large, still look strictly for that.

Attracting employees with challenges, providing the opportunity to work with innovative products or services, and offering any or all of the above-mentioned pluses are only part of the picture of keeping good employees. The personality of the business owner should be the guiding force that makes the company attractive to employees, but maintaining morale and satisfaction over time are management skills that not all entrepreneurs have. This is due to the fact that dynamic leadership and ingenuity do not necessarily equal good management. Further, the added dimension of cross-cultural relationships compounds the management challenge.

## RUNNING A BICULTURAL OFFICE

"It's usually a *gaijin* [foreigner]-Japanese problem with employees, but somehow, you work it out," said Claus Regge of Soundwork, Inc. and Network, Inc., both companies employing a total of 16 employees. The company and its well-being are always more important than daily, petty squabbles, and talking things over is one way to resolve differences.

For other companies, problems can be more severe, requiring more than "talking things over." Witan Associates, a corporate communications firm, experienced a culture-clash dilemma that threatened to completely disrupt the business after only two years in operation. The challenge arose to "create a fair and productive work environment for people from both Japanese and Western cultures," according to one of the partners, "because organization building became as important as completing work assignments."

The company embarked on a program to clearly delineate company goals, implementing decisions biculturally, rather than in an authoritarian manner as had been done previously. Most importantly, the 25-person company learned true biculturality, which is not only a function of language facility, something that every staff member had, but involved becoming aware of differences in values and thinking about that factor before communicating with each other. Open discussion of problems was encouraged, rather than deferring the issues to a later date.

The training program allowed for a venting of frustrations and differences, facilitated by an interpreter, to get a 100% accurate picture of trouble spots. "People realized how many things they had been misinterpreting as a result of simple language problems. People said things on that first day (of the training program) that they might never have had the courage to say in the company."

Furthermore, by gearing compensation to productivity, employees began to feel responsible for work results. Setting new goals every six months and evaluating performance records also helped the company and the employees to control actions and see the actual returns on time and effort. These actions also helped Witan Associates to develop into a more structured enterprise, rather than remain a family-type business. Ms. Cramer attributes the subsequent 20% increase in sales to participation in this program and the company now has an ongoing series of bicultural meetings.

Corporate awareness training programs and incentive bonuses seem to be equally motivating for Japanese and foreign employees. Further, interdependent jobs that require mutual cooperation have allowed small businesses to foster motivation and employee morale as well as cooperation between foreigners and Japanese. (There are evidently some fields where incentive pay is difficult to implement, however. Thomas Caldwell of Caldwell & Associates noted that the commission system is not appealing to route salesmen in Japan, who prefer a straight salary.)

A relevant comment on bicultural offices comes from Thomas Nevins, president of TMT, Inc., a management consulting firm, who observed that 50% of motivation problems are foreign management's fault, but another 50% stem from Japanese workers blaming their unproductivity on having to work in a foreign enterprise, a rationalization.

## FULL-TIME VS. PART-TIME EMPLOYEES

In Japan, employees are divided into three classifications with the corresponding duties and obligations of employee and employer determined thereby. The *seishain* or full-time employee; the *arubaito* or part-timer, and the *keiyaku (shokutaku),* or contract employee, comprise the three groups. Foreign employees often choose the last categorization, according to some of the surveyed businesses, since social welfare benefits need not be paid to the employee, unless contracted for, and so withholding tax is lower for the employee.

**Details on Full-timers.** Because hiring an employee under *seishain* status guarantees security to the employee, firing is made next to impossible without incurring heavy financial and legal liability. Discriminatory hiring of Japanese employees and a three-month probationary period are therefore advisable.

Bob White of ARC International, a personnel management and

consulting firm, has stated that hiring unnecessary personnel is taboo, since employees cannot be easily disposed of when a business
cycle is down. "When you fire someone, it's viewed as a breach
of trust; the other employees get shaky and quit as a result." In
the 11-year history of the company, now a large enterprise, only
two people have been fired, one of whom brought legal action that
threatened to bankrupt the firm. Other business owners complained
of lazy secretaries and assistants whom they wanted to fire, but due
to the legal considerations, they were simply unable to do so.

The payment of bonuses, paid holidays, social welfare benefits,
and retirement allowances are the financial advantages accruing
to full-time employees, but more importantly, the status of being
a full-timer and the feeling of belonging to the enterprise team is
of paramount importance to the Japanese employee. (If a company
has five or more Japanese full-time employees, social insurance,
including national health and welfare compensation and employment insurance, must be offered by the employer.)

Perhaps the amount of obligations owed to full-time employees
has influenced some entrepreneurs to do as German art-book dealer Klaus Stiebling has. "I have no employees. I do it all by myself."

**Part-timers.**    It is thus preferable to employ part-timers, due to
the flexibility that the classification offers to both employer and employee. Part-timer, however, does not mirror the U.S. concept, as
many in Japan work a forty-hour week and stay with a company
over a span of years. For example, in 1986, 4.7 million part-timers
worked on the average for 3.9 years at a job—hardly part-time.

The *arubaito*—from the German word *arbeit* [work], adapted to
mean part-time employment in Japan—has recently become the
object of controversy, particularly in regard to those who work long-
term for a company on what appears to be a full-time basis but
who have little protection under the law concerning benefits, wage
increases, bonuses, and promotions. A 1984 government directive

promulgated to encourage businesses to give part-timers more benefits, regular salary increases, and promotions does not have the force of law, so temporary manpower services have become a thriving business due to the lack of legal obligations and constraints on employers. Another reason for the boom in temporary employees is that Japanese women now want to work part-time due to changing sex roles and an increasing desire for self-actualization.

Many temporary workers have complained that their employers exploit them, forcing them to work long overtime hours without remuneration, but that the work cannot be refused because the workers are not union members. At a recent Labor Ministry symposium sponsored to promote the acceptance of the 1984 guidelines, these problems were discussed. The Labor Ministry has, as a result, requested employers to improve conditions for part-timers to ensure job security for the many housewives who are a source of cheap labor for the business community.

Part-timers working five days a week or more at the same place are entitled to paid holidays, and employers must provide health checks, but the use of these workers in vaguely defined categories allows employers to skirt these mandates. The law also supposedly requires that office workers can only work for nine months at a temporary job, although this proviso is not enforced as to small businesses due to the ambiguous classification of workers and the sheer number of small businesses in existence.

Since temporary workers are dispatched according to the requirements of the employer, one entrepreneur has suggested that the temporary service be informed from the beginning of the length of time that the worker's services will be needed. This is especially important since many Japanese temporary workers are employed by several agencies, so the worker should be "reserved" if there is a long-term job to be performed. If, for example, a better working opportunity arises with another temporary company, the worker will take it, if no agreement has been reached. To avoid wasting time reacclimating and retraining someone, an agreement for a specific period of time should be made.

Two temporary manpower companies that have been recommended are:

> Manpower Japan Co., Ltd.
> No. 3 Kowa Bldg.
> 1-11-45 Akasaka
> Minato-ku, Tokyo 107
> Tel: (03) 582-1761

> Adia Japan Ltd.
> Sanpo-Akasaka Bldg. 4F
> 2-5-7 Akasaka
> Minato-ku, Tokyo 107
> Tel: (03) 505-3241 (Akasaka)
> Tel: (03) 575-4840 (Ginza)

## A NOTE ON THE EQUAL OPPORTUNITY LAW

An Equal Opportunity Law went into effect on April 1, 1986, its objective being the banning of discriminatory treatment of women by reason of sex as to employee training, welfare benefits, retirement age, and discharge. It also calls for companies "to make every effort" to ensure equal treatment in recruitment, employment, promotion, and job assignment. Liberalization of the number of hours of overtime that a woman is allowed to do is also another objective of the law. However, no penalties are present for not complying with these recommendations.

Since most part-timers are women, the law is certainly pertinent, and although it does not delineate penalties for non-compliance, it is expected to change the character of the Japanese workplace. Prospective employers, large and small, should be aware of the indirect influence of the law on the expectations of Japanese women in the job market.

## WORK RULES AND PENSIONS

**Work Rules.**   If a company has 10 or more Japanese employees, work rules must be composed. Work rules should provide the basics on the style of work, expected performance, adherence to company precepts, administrative duties, working hours, vacations, and disciplinary action.

**Pensions.**   Adopting a pension plan for one's employees is a good idea, but businesses, especially smaller ones, often do not perceive the need for one. A pension plan system creates the appearance of a stable work atmosphere and a desire for long-term presence in Japan.

Pension plans can be funded by the company or financed through retained earnings or by a loan from a bank or insurance company. Those financed directly are called straight-funding programs and those achieved through loans from an insurance company are called "unqualified" plans. Instead of having a pension plan, many companies pay bonuses for successful performance based on corporate results. This method works to keep the employees of small businesses happy, since many of them are foreign nationals who are usually not in Japan for the long haul, and so are not concerned with pension pay-offs to be made in the distant future.

## ON THE COST OF EMPLOYEES

The following figures will clearly demonstrate the expense involved in hiring good personnel in Japan. According to the Labor Ministry, the nominal average monthly wage of workers in 1985 was ¥317,138, rising 3.6% from 1984. Of the total monthly wages paid to workers in cash, the fixed amount, including base pay and regular allowances, averaged ¥236,593, for an increase of 4% over 1984. Average bonuses and other special remuneration paid out in 1985 totaled ¥966,540, or a total monthly average of ¥85,415, an increase of 2.6% since 1984.

The average number of working hours on a monthly basis in 1985 was 175.8, a decrease of 0.8% from 1984, with the monthly number of working days in 1985 averaging in at 21.8. Required working hours averaged 160 hours; overtime working hours averaged 14.8 hours, an increase of 1.5% over 1984. (The number of overtime working hours is noteworthy, however, because a regular five-day workweek has yet to be fully instituted in Japan in either the government or private sectors.)

It is obvious that employee costs are one reason small companies attempt to engage as few people as possible, especially full-time workers. Small businesses need to target the three special types of employees outlined above, who may be interested in non-monetary benefits and opportunities, or use part-timers, which involves less commitment as to salary, raises, bonuses, promotions, job security, health insurance benefits, transportation allowances, housing and family support, retirement benefits, and business trip expenses.

# 8

# Costs of Doing Business

Tokyo has been rated as the most expensive place in the world. That's why finding the right office or shop location takes investigative prowess and money. Aside from labor costs, the costs of establishing a business outlet or office are so high that 10 of the business people interviewed chose to operate out of their homes, since by doing so they were able to deduct part of their rent as expenses. One man did note, however, that business and family "do not mix."

## FINDING A SUITABLE LOCATION

The reasons for the choice of office location usually centered on price, explaining the location of many offices of entrepreneurs in less than prime areas. However, other reasons included the need to be near suppliers or services, or the ability to accomodate deliveries and pick-ups. Also, when clients did not come to the office because there was a sales force servicing the customer, a less prestigious office environment was acceptable.

Michael Dunn, an art/antique dealer, mentioned that most good art dealers were operating on a private basis, not showing at the galleries, and he felt that the appointment-required aspect of his business was a must for prestige imagery. Therefore, operating out of his residence presented no problems.

Being close to major clients is another consideration that was important to several business owners, but other, more unusual reasons for office location were also present. "Shibuya (a district in Tokyo) is a young people's town," said Fran Kuzui of Kuzui Enterprises, a film distribution and promotion company. "When we had a chance to move into an office here because a Japanese company took an interest in working with us and located the space, we couldn't refuse." She obtained access to a phone, a telex, the contemporary Japanese youth scene outside of her window, and a space next to her benefactor. The nominal rent that the Japanese company offered her sealed the first step to commitment as business allies.

André Pachon, restauranteur, received an invitation to locate his second restaurant in a high-class building in Daikanyama, another trendy area. Since he was requested to move there by the owner, he did not have to pay a large deposit on the space, a standard Japanese practice. He says, "Mine was a special case: not paying a deposit and being invited by the building owner."

Amaury St. Gilles, art gallery proprietor, wanted space and a particular mood for his business, although he acknowledged it is not conveniently located for most of the expatriate community. His gallery is a renovated pawn broker's shop that is roomy and very Japanese in feeling, a characteristic which he could not easily obtain in today's Tokyo.

Some proprietors make lucky deals. Jane Yonamine was offered a tailor's backroom, and when the man went bankrupt, she took over. The owner of the building was a sympathetic woman who helped her by not raising the rent for several months until the business advanced. She is still in the same place twenty years later.

## OFFICE RENTAL COSTS/OFFICE VACANCY RATES

In order to comprehend the expensive chore of opening an office in Tokyo, you should refer to the statistics on page 96, from a survey compiled by the Japan Building Managers and Owners Association in 1985. Of 266 offices surveyed, those in the Marunouchi district had the most expensive office rents—23 offices with an

# A Comparison of Building Rental Costs (According to Location)

(Calculated in units—unit = ¥100)

¥2,000 … ¥14,500

| District | 20~25 | 25~30 | 30~35 | 35~40 | 40~45 | 45~50 | 50~55 | 55~60 | 60~65 | 65~70 | 70~75 | 75~80 | 80~85 | 85~90 | 90~95 | 95~100 | 100~105 | 105~110 | 110~115 | 115~120 | 120~125 | 125~130 | 130~135 | 135~140 | 140~145 | Total | Average Monthly Rent Per Sq. Meter |
|---|---|---|---|---|---|---|---|---|---|---|---|---|---|---|---|---|---|---|---|---|---|---|---|---|---|---|---|
| Marunouchi District | | | | | | | | | | | | | 1 | | | | 1 | 3 | 2 | | 3 | 6 | 23 | 2 | | 41 | ¥12,647 |
| Kanda District | | 2 | 2 | 3 | 3 | 4 | 5 | 1 | 5 | 3 | | | | | | | | | | | | | | | | 28 | 5,561 |
| Kasumigaseki District | | | | | | | | | | | | | | | | | | 2 | 2 | 2 | 1 | 1 | 1 | | 1 | 10 | 10,444 |
| Nihonbashi District | | 1 | 2 | | 3 | 1 | 6 | 7 | 2 | 3 | 2 | 1 | 3 | 2 | 1 | 1 | 3 | | | | | 1 | | | | 39 | 6,549 |
| Ginza District | | 1 | | | 3 | 4 | 4 | 4 | 2 | 1 | | 1 | 3 | 1 | 1 | | 1 | | | | | | | | | 26 | 6,033 |
| Shinbashi District | | | | 1 | 2 | 2 | 3 | 2 | 5 | 1 | 7 | 6 | 1 | 4 | 1 | 3 | 1 | | | | | 1 | | | | 40 | 7,164 |
| Akasaka District | 1 | | | | 2 | 2 | 2 | 2 | 1 | 1 | | 1 | | 3 | | 1 | | | | | | | | | | 16 | 6,349 |
| Shinjuku-ku | | | 3 | 2 | 4 | 2 | | 4 | | | | 2 | | 2 | | 2 | | | | | | | | | | 21 | 5,641 |
| Shibuya-ku | | 1 | 3 | 1 | 1 | 2 | 1 | 4 | 3 | 2 | | 1 | | 1 | 1 | | | | | | | | | | | 21 | 5,551 |
| Toshima-ku | | | | | | 1 | | 1 | | | | 1 | | | | | | | | | | | | | | 3 | 5,855 |
| Other | 1 | | 5 | 5 | 4 | 6 | | | | | | | | | | | | | | | | | | | | 21 | 4,022 |
| Total | 2 | 5 | 15 | 12 | 22 | 24 | 21 | 25 | 18 | 11 | 9 | 13 | 8 | 13 | 4 | 7 | 6 | 5 | 4 | 2 | 4 | 9 | 24 | 2 | 1 | 266 | 7,204 |

Note: Monthly rental charge is calculated by adding the basic rental charge to the deposit and dividing that amount by 12.
(Monthly Amount = Rent + Deposit (*shikikin* or *hoshokin*) ÷ 12.  Rent + (*shikikin* × 10% + *hoshokin* × (10% − interest) ÷ 12)

average monthly rent of ¥13,000–13,500 per square meter of space. The least expensive offices were in the last category typed as "Other," located in other than prime downtown locations and ranging from ¥2,000–2,500 per square meter, still hefty sums. Overall, most offices are clustered in the ¥4,000–7,000 per square meter range, although more expensive space than that is quite conspicuous.

While the prime locations of Shibuya, Shinjuku, and Kanda do, however, evidence a sizable proportion of office space in the lower-priced categories, averaging in at ¥5,551, ¥5,641, and ¥5,561 per square meter respectively, upon calculation of the total monthly rent, the illusion of "a good bargain" quickly disappears. For example, an average 10 *tsubo* (33 square meters or about 39 square yards) office in Shinjuku would cost ¥186,153 per month. (One *tsubo* equals 3.3 square meters and is the equivalent of two *tatami* mats. Space is usually quantified in terms of "mats" or *tsubo*.) These exorbitant office space costs are clearly a handicap for small business owners.

The chart on page 98 shows the trends in the vacancy rate for office space in Japan over the years. (This chart was also compiled by the Japan Building Managers and Owners Association in 1985.) By following the bottom line, which represents Tokyo, it can be seen that from the high point of a 23.6% vacancy rate in 1976, the rate continued to drop to a low of 11% in 1985, the lowest vacancy rate since 1973. Tokyo office space is an increasingly hard-to-come-by commodity. It remains to be seen whether recent plans to move government offices to the suburbs of Tokyo will go ahead, and whether this strategy will help to ease the real estate crisis.

## RETAIL SHOP RENTAL COSTS

For those considering rental of shop space for a retail business enterprise, the list on page 99 of costs in four fashionable Tokyo locations will demonstrate how expensive it is.

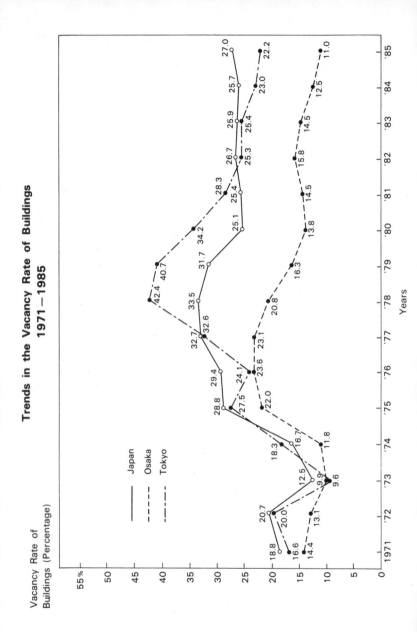

Trends in the Vacancy Rate of Buildings
1971–1985

Vacancy Rate of
Buildings (Percentage)

Years

Japan
Osaka
Tokyo

|                                | RENT        | DEPOSIT       |
|--------------------------------|-------------|---------------|
| Aoyama (From First Building)   | ¥25–35,000  | ¥200–250,000  |
| Harajuku                       | ¥20–35,000  | ¥250–300,000  |
| Nishi Azabu                    | ¥35–40,000  | ¥300–350,000  |
| (Junko Koshino Shop)           |             |               |
| Daikanyama                     | ¥35–40,000  | ¥250–300,000  |

**Note:** These rent prices pertain to 1 *tsubo* of space.

A five *tsubo* shop (16.5 square meters) would cost approximately ¥150,000 per month in, for example, the Harajuku district with an initial required deposit (*shikikin* or *hoshōkin*) of ¥1,500,000. While the rent may not be extremely expensive, the deposit is. (In central Tokyo, business space deposits are often equal to 10–12 months of rent and can easily reach 24 months!)

**DETAILS ON THE RENT**

Rent (*chinryō*) is calculated from the move-in date specified in the lease. If the office must be remodeled, painted, etc. before moving in, it is calculated from the day that the place is actually used.

Rent is usually paid between the 25th and the last day of the month for the next month, but rent for a period of less than a month can be prorated.

When a lease comes up for renewal, usually every two years, many landlords request a raise in the rent because of the skyrocketing price of land in Tokyo. This is a bitter pill that a tenant must often swallow since moving means incurring greater expense, as new security deposits must be paid. Some contracts, as Sanko Real Estate Company has noted, do specify that renewal during the term of the lease can only be accomplished after mutual agreement of the parties involved, and higher rent for the renewal term can be limited to the following cases:

1. when taxes or other financial obligtions on the building have increased;
2. when inflation affects the price of various goods;
3. when the current rent is different from that of other buildings in the area.

However, since any of the conditions can be claimed with some accuracy, these provisions do not seem to aid business tenants.

A rent renewal fee *(kōshinryō)* must usually be paid upon renewal of the lease by the lessee, and is equivalent to at least one month's rent, but sometimes more. It is non-refundable.

Always remember that rents for a Tokyo office depend on the age of the building and its location, that is, whether it is in a central or peripheral spot, and that ground floor space is 3–4 times more expensive.

It should be mentioned at this point that finder's fees for realtors are standard and are at least the equivalent of one month's rent. This charge cannot usually be escaped, since 90% of rentals take place through a realtor.

## DEPOSITS

In Japanese, a security deposit is called *hoshōkin* or *shikikin*. These are non-interest deposits payable to the landlord by the lessee to provide a guarantee against delinquent payment of rent, damage to the property, etc. The lessee cannot assign the right to the deposit money to a third party or use it as security for other obligations or demand that the money be applied toward rent due.

*Hoshōkin* was originally a building construction aid sought by owners after World War II. The need for such capital has abated, but the practice of getting it has not. *Shikikin,* however, is to ensure that the landlord is paid if the lessee defaults on payment of rent or other obligations.

While *hoshōkin* is refundable at the end of the lease, *shikikin* is not. *Hoshōkin-henkan,* or return of the deposit money, is effected after the premises are returned to the lessor in their original condition *(genjō kaifuku),* which means all fixtures and equipment installed or added must be removed. If there is any money owed to the lessor after the premises are returned to him, or if the lessee fails to restore the premises to the original condition, the amounts can be deducted from the *hoshōkin.* It is also customary to deduct 10–20% from the *hoshōkin* as a depreciation fee. The tenant does not receive much, if any, of his "building construction aid" deposit back.

## MAINTENANCE FEES

Aside from the deposits and the monthly rent, office space renters must also pay a monthly maintenance fee *(kyōekihi),* differing from case to case but usually ranging from ¥3,000–7,500 per *tsubo.* Moreover, utilities, ventilation charges, cleaning, window washing charges, water bills, and design and renovation costs are, of course, separate from maintenance charges, and all add up.

The cost of utilities for the common facilities in an office building is usually included in the lease, but the costs of energy and water consumed within individual offices are billed to the tenants. Water rates in Tokyo depend on the diameter of the pipes, which is determined by the building's size. Monthly electricity rates also depend on the size of the building.

While maintenance fees for the common areas usually include utilities, this is not always the case. Maintenance fees sometimes only include expenses for the entrance hall, elevators, and hallways, and exclude utilities, so the contract should be checked in each case.

Signboard user fees are also charged to tenants.

The chart on the following page is a breakdown of the types of maintenance costs and other monthly charges for tenants of office buildings in Tokyo. (This chart courtesy of Sanko Real Estate Company.)

# COSTS

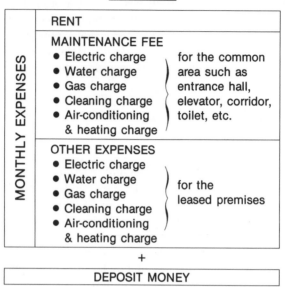

| | |
|---|---|
| **MONTHLY EXPENSES** | **RENT** |
| | **MAINTENANCE FEE**<br>• Electric charge<br>• Water charge<br>• Gas charge<br>• Cleaning charge<br>• Air-conditioning & heating charge  — for the common area such as entrance hall, elevator, corridor, toilet, etc. |
| | **OTHER EXPENSES**<br>• Electric charge<br>• Water charge<br>• Gas charge<br>• Cleaning charge<br>• Air-conditioning & heating charge  — for the leased premises |

+

**DEPOSIT MONEY**

## REMODELING

Remodeling, rewiring, telephone installation, lighting, and furniture/interior decoration are all services provided by interior decorators. These services usually cost at least ¥500,000 for a 10-mat (*jō*) space or five *tsubo* area. Decorators charge 5–15% of the total cost of construction.

## REPAIRS

Repairs (*shūzenhi*) are divided between the lessor and lessee, but a lessor must repair the building structure, ceiling, walls, floor, or anything related to the building structure, common areas, and equipment. Lessees must assume liability for, and repair, partitions, fixtures, equipment exclusively used by the lessee, blinds, light bulbs, switches, and electrical outlets of the leased premises, as well as the ceiling, walls, and floor of the leased premises.

Even if the lessee wants to repair the premises, fixtures, or equipment at his own expense, permission should be obtained from the lessor first.

Lessees should always find out the rules of the building owner concerning repairs in advance, as these vary greatly.

## PROHIBITION OF SUBLETTING AND ASSIGNMENT

Usually, lessees cannot reassign the lease or sublet the leased premises, use the premises as security, or transfer any of the rights under the lease.

Furthermore, the lessee cannot co-occupy the leased premises or allow another to warrant that the premises are his place of business, unless the lessor consents. If a party is financially related to the lessee, the lessor may sometimes allow co-occupancy.

## NOTICE OF CANCELLATION OF LEASE

If a lessee wants to terminate the lease during the lease term, the lessee must give advance notice, usually six months prior to termination. If the lessee wants to cancel without prior notice, a penalty must be paid, sometimes equal to six months' rent.

## MANAGEMENT CONTROL RULES

Administrative regulations *(kanri kisoku)* concern the daily management of the building, including opening and closing hours, regular air-conditioning and heating hours, use of the building beyond regular hours, working hours of janitors, regulations for keys, etc. These should be checked in advance, since they differ widely.

## A TRUE STORY ABOUT RENTING OFFICE SPACE

Reiko Lyster of Elle International related a troubling account of renting office space.

When her business began to expand and new office space was needed, she began to office hunt. After finding a suitable location, she wanted to lease the premises promptly, but when the owner of the building, a major Japanese construction company, learned that she was not a Japanese citizen, she was told that she could not lease the office without the signature of a Japanese national who was neither an employee nor a relative. This requirement was in addition to the requirement of a personal guarantor.

As Ms. Lyster said, "What was was so ridiculous about the whole affair was that my firm was already paying rent for three other locations in an amount five times in excess of that in dispute." She ultimately decided not to yield to such an annoyance and found another office.

## AN ALTERNATIVE TO THE OFFICE BUILDING CRUNCH

One way to avoid the high cost of office space is to convert an apartment into an office. Apartment building owners usually ask for a non-refundable deposit *(reikin)* and one, two, or even three months' rent as a refundable deposit *(shikikin)*. The small business can take advantage of this option and escape the variety of "miscellaneous charges."

When one rents an apartment in Tokyo, the following amounts of money must be paid for an average 10-*tsubo* apartment (33 square meters):

1. Gift to the landlord *(reikin)*:    one or two months' rent (¥250,000)

2. Refundable deposit *(shikikin)*:    one or two months' rent (¥250,000)

| | |
|---|---|
| 3. Monthly rent: | ¥125,000 |
| 4. Monthly maintenance fee: | ¥10,000 |
| 5. Realtor's fee: | ¥125,000 (usually equal to one month's rent) |
| TOTAL: | ¥760,000 (includes first month's rent) |

The renter would have to put out six months' rent at first, which is a sizeable expense, but the monthly rent is substantially cheaper than standard office charges. However, remember that a rental renewal fee is charged when the lease is renewed and is non-refundable, ranging from one to three months' rent.

Using one's home as an office space may not only be cheaper, but it is also partially a deductible expense for tax purposes. That is why so many small business owners or those just starting out choose this form of business location.

### LEASING OFFICE EQUIPMENT

Office machines can be leased or purchased, but leasing contracts are usually longer than rental contracts, running for 3–5 years on average while the latter run for about a year or less. Renting costs more than leasing, although rental contracts can be canceled at any time; canceling a lease contract is more costly.

Provisos on leasing are highlighted by the following stories. When Bunny Cramer of Witan Associates attempted to lease a copy machine, she was told that unless a Japanese male guarantor signed on her behalf, there could be no lease. This was in spite of the fact that she had a Japanese woman partner and the lease was only for ¥9,000 per month. Kerry Kennedy, a marketing research consultant, related that because he was well aware of the difficulty of leasing from Japanese companies, he chose to deal with another foreign entrepreneur to obtain his computer set-up.

Leases usually have three parties to the contract: the user, the manufacturer, and the lease company. The user pays the lease company monthly payments amounting to about 120% of the cost of the equipment. (The cost is equal to the equipment price, insurance, tax, interest, and the lease company's fee.)

Since lease payments are 100% tax deductible, leases are more advantageous than outright purchases. Only the depreciation rate and interest are tax deductible for purchases.

## TEMPORARY OFFICE SPACE

Several businesses in Tokyo now offer use of facilities and access to secretarial help, phones, message services, fax and telex services, conference rooms, etc. The advantage of sharing office costs and secretarial services is in cutting costs. For those with the means, the temporary office space concept is fine, but for smaller entrepreneurs, who need an office they can use on a daily basis, it may not suit their requirements or their budget.

For example, Jardine Matheson's "Identity Plan" is convenient for those who want to maintain a private Tokyo address while on the road or prior to office establishment. The service provides a businessman with a phone, telex, fax, receptionist, message service, private mailbox, a mail-handling service, and a lobby directory listing for ¥440,000 for a 12-month period. When in Tokyo, temporary office space, conference rooms, and secretaries are available at extra cost. The following list is a breakdown of some of the extra fees involved:

| | |
|---|---|
| bilingual secretarial service: | ¥5,000/hour |
| word processing/typing: | ¥1,500/double spaced |
| | ¥2,500/single spaced |
| conference room: | room available to plan members at ¥5,000/hour (subject to availability) |

While a variety of services and plans are offered, this office service center is not inexpensive, and seems best to use on a temporary basis. (A temporary office space costs ¥10,000–35,000 per day.)

Jardine Business Center Tokyo
ABS Building
2-4-16 Kudan Minami
Chiyoda-ku, Tokyo 102
Tel: (03) 239-2811
Fax: (03) 239-2817
Telex: J32384

The Tokyo International Business Center (TIBC) in Shiba Daimon close to Tokyo tower advertises itself as "office space for small businesses," and offers four-meter-square office spaces for ¥200,000/month. To use the space you need to purchase a four-year membership (nonrefundable) for ¥50,000, and to make a deposit of ¥200,000 (refundable). Each office has a desk, telephone, and stationary provided, while word processors and fax machines are shared with other tenants. There is an English-speaking receptionist, answering service, mail-routing service, business information service, schedule administration service, soft-drinks service, and reception room included in the membership. (Telephone charges are based on actual use.) The TIBC offers many other services on an "actual cost" basis, including copying, telex, typing and secretarial services, introduction to domestic business concerns, credit information, etc.

Tokyo International Business Center, Inc.
Tobe Building, 4th Floor
2-9-17 Shiba Daimon,
Minato-ku, Tokyo 105
Tel: (03) 578-9002
Fax: (03) 578-9011
Telex: 242-7558

The Australian Business Center (ABC) offers office and meeting facilities for ¥300,000/year. The service includes telex, copier, fax, after-hours telephone service, and bilingual secretaries. For more information on what the Australian Business Center has to offer, call (03) 470-1018.

ABC
Watanabe Bldg. 4th Floor
1-4-2 Minami Aoyama
Minato-ku, Tokyo 107

## "INCUBATOR INTERNATIONAL"

Run by an entrepreneur with 34 years of business experience in Japan, this operation assists medium-sized companies to start operations in Japan.

Willi Thaler's concept centers on the reality that it takes around $400,000 (U.S.) a year for three years before an enterprise is in the black or even viable. While many smaller businesses do survive and succeed in Japan, for those with more capital seeking to get into the market, Thaler will act as the Japanese office. He emphasizes that he is not an agent since he requires an investment of about $150,000 (U.S.) from a business and a three-year commitment.

What does a business get in return? An experienced manager, as well as accounting, storage of inventory and distribution, export-import services, and secretarial staff.

Low-risk investment for market entry and starting a business in Japan: not a bad deal for the small-to-medium venture from overseas knocking on Japan's door.

## INSURANCE

The protection of one's business assets from fire and natural disaster by taking out property and casualty insurance on an "all-risk" policy is the way to go, say the small business experts. According to Dave Wouters of Wouters & Associates, representing AIU insurance company in Japan, the all-risk policy covers movables, whether rented or purchased, all office equipment, furniture, paneling, and carpeting.

Trade inventory can be insured under an all-risk policy as well, and the rate is basically the same as for a policy insuring office assets alone. Both types of all-risk policies are cheaper than U.S. equivalents, because there are fewer cases of stolen property in Japan, so assets can be insured at lower rates due to less risk.

As for earthquake insurance, however, major insurance companies do not handle it in Japan because the risk is too high and it cannot easily be reinsured since too many people want coverage and the market is "saturated." However, Wouters stated that he can obtain all-risk property and casualty insurance coverage that includes damage due to earthquakes.

Immovables can be insured, but renters of office space do not require this type of coverage and usually choose to purchase fire/legal liability insurance instead. That is, if the tenant causes a fire and the landlord sues the tenant for damages, the policy covers the insured for any claims that must be paid to the building owner.

# 9

# Advertising

## A FEW WORDS ABOUT JAPANESE ETIQUETTE

*Meishi.*   The Japanese businessman who does not have a *meishi* in his pocket is a rare breed indeed. *Meishi,* or business cards, are used in the millions every day in Japan and function as ID cards, listing name, address, phone number, and title or position. The title or position of the giver is the most important item, perhaps, since it will determine the level of polite Japanese to be used and what amount of deference/respect is owed to him.

*Meishi* are a "security blanket" of sorts since they serve to identify a person's place in the corporate world and society at large, the company being the touchstone of personal identity for the usual Japanese salaryman. It has actually been stated that the Japanese are not really confident without the card, since a lone individual without a corporate home is an outcast.

The following is an interesting excerpt from a *Washington Post* article by John Burgess:

> Foreigners never quite master the etiquette of *meishi* exchange, no matter how many times they do it. Japanese often get it right only through formal instruction as company trainees. . . . With one hand, the giver deftly produces from a pocket the special folder . . . with the other, he deals out one with a crisp little snap of the wrist, something like a casino dealer's. Simultaneously, he calls out his name and makes a brief bow.
>
> It is bad form simply to pocket a newly received card. You should study it for a moment with a furrowed look of interest.

Any notes you want to scribble on it to help you remember the new acquaintance must wait until he is gone. The next time you meet him, you must not offer a card again, because that would mean you had forgotten him.

To snub someone, you can take his card and offer none in return, without explanation. Businessmen sometimes complain they get this treatment from bureaucrats. You have thus established that he is the inferior.

***Nenga-jō.*** The exchange of New Year's greeting cards, or *nenga-jō*, is the second form of politeness that should be observed. These postcard-like greetings are sent out in volume by Japanese businessmen, and foreigners should also cultivate the habit, as many interviewees have noted. As one said, "Send your *nenga-jō* every year to your Japanese clients and even if you don't speak for a few years, you'll always have those ties that mean so much in Japan."

One last point about *nenga-jō,* however, is that sending these cards is like eating potato chips: you may start with a few, but then you can't stop. It's considered bad form to send out cards and then fail to continue doing so, as it is a direct slight to the receiver.

***O-Chugen* and *O-Seibo.*** These are the gifts that are given at mid-year and at the end of the year, respectively. The former is especially for presenting gifts to thank someone for having "taken care of you" in business for the period of time from January through July. The season runs from about the end of June to mid-July. "Summer gifts" are sent by all good Japanese businessmen. The *o-seibo* season is December and again the proper presents are always sent, including salad oil, seaweed, soaps, liquor, or fruit.

While you may be anxious to create a Japanese image, it is suggested that you do not be too hasty to send these gifts. Instead, please send your *nenga-jō,* as stated above, and Christmas and birthday cards to the key men on your list of Japanese clients, customers, suppliers, etc. Doing so will allow you to develop the personal relations *(ningen kankei)*, which are paramount, while still maintaining your foreign identity, your best "charm point" in Japan. Anyway, as a Japanese businessman stated, " . . . the *o-chugen/o-seibo* gift-giving process is too traditionally Japanese and is too brown-nosing and humbling, even for us."

To maintain your personal relations, an alternative suggestion is to spend your money on wining and dining your key Japanese contacts. Taking them to dinner in place of the seasonal gifts is as effective a device as gift-giving, and keeps you out of the "gift-giving rat race," something you don't absolutely have to participate in.

## BUSINESS CONTACTS/PERSONAL CONNECTIONS

Advertising for the foreign small business in Japan means more than educating the public about one's products or services. It means cultivating personal contacts and ties by using references and personal entrées, and establishing more contacts to reap the benefits of sales/billings. While advertising usually means direct mail, point-of-sale promotion, seminars, samples of merchandise, demonstrations, or print advertisements, in Japan, it more frequently denotes handing out numerous *meishi* (business cards), getting to know dealers, customers, and distributors, and socializing with them to build credibility and familiarity. As one entrepreneur has suggested, a *meishi* is the best advertising for the least amount of money.

Since trust is not readily accorded to a foreigner in business in Japan (it comes only after long-term relationships have been formed), the small, foreign businessman must work doubly hard to establish confidence and show a willingness to adapt products or services to the marketplace. This is because the small firm does not have the visibility or prestige of a larger company, or ready access to upper echelon or government personnel, which the Japanese businessman respects so greatly. The small business must, therefore, mobilize its uniqueness and promote its positive differences.

Early establishment and continued presence lead to the cultivation of ties and recognition of one's credibility, musts for doing business in Japan. Only one-third of the businessmen and businesswomen interviewed use advertising of the conventional type, that is, newspaper/magazine ads, promotions, direct mail, or point-of-purchase incentives. The other two-thirds rely on alternatives, such as handing out numerous *meishi* and cultivating contacts on a word-of-mouth basis. An agent for a German beer dispenser was able to hook up with Kirin Beer, for example, due to his accumulation of personal contacts. Kirin provided the distribution network while the company in Germany paid only for the ads. However, even without such "tie-in" arrangements, one can succeed.

Repeatedly, entrepreneurs stressed the need for good personal introductions as opposed to "cold calling." One businessman stated that 90% of his billings come from client introductions, since cold calls rarely work in Japan and are never as effective as introductions. Other businessmen detailed how their enterprises began with personal friends as customers, and that praise for their services or products became the accepted way of advertising for them. For example, Jane Yonamine of Yonamine Pearls started buying pearls for friends in Hawaii over 22 years ago, which blossomed into a full-time business in Japan. She does not advertise, nor does she have to, as word-of-mouth has garnered her over 40 suppliers and wholesalers, well over ¥30 million in earnings per year, and clients like the top brass in major corporations.

Mary-Jane Connelly, advertising manager of International Technical Trading, Inc., a trading company that imports housewares and sporting goods, emphasized that personal presence over time at trade shows and developing contacts by personally demonstrating the products, not through hired help or agents, are the most memorable forms of establishing business contacts.

## NEWSPAPERS/TRADE ADVERTISING

It is difficult to buy space in Japanese newspapers, since advertising space is limited to 20 pages per issue, meaning space must be booked way ahead of time, even though there are over 16,000 newspapers in Japan! Thus, only large advertising companies or those with an inside line can buy space. An example of the latter is Australian entrepreneur Terrie Lloyd's Linc Japan, Ltd., an advertising agency that can buy space in the Nikkei group of papers. However, as Lloyd has stated, "Newspapers are not the best way to advertise products, unless wide readership is desired."

Magazines and trade papers are tailored to a narrower audience than newspapers, so are more effective for reaching highly segmented portions of the Japanese populace. An interesting tip on magazines related by Lloyd is that the price of magazine space can be bargained for, because the length of an advertisement can be expanded, unlike in a newspaper. Also, because many magazines have a transient life, they are eager to grab advertising clientele. (Dummy ads, or those free of charge, are offered to big companies, which allows the magazine, if it gets a few nibbles on its offer, to claim those big advertisers as references.)

As for ads in trade journals, these are utilized more by small businesses than newspaper and magazine ads because of the relative inexpensiveness and ability to reach a more segmented target audience. As for specialty items, Claus Regge advertises his quality European oboes in musicians' periodicals on a regular basis because his client base is small: professional oboe players. Advertising directed solely at the wholesale trade is attributable to the fact that many small businesses are wholesalers, so that tapping into other Japanese wholesalers who have distribution link-ups and ties with retailers is key. Dick Adler of Corton Trading reported spending ¥1 million per month on slick ads in trade journals.

One business owner stated that although he used to advertise regularly in magazines, he found that sales were better when appointments were scheduled, so he stopped advertising. "When advertising while you own a shop in Japan, people get the impression that items become more expensive, which they do, due to high overhead." Word-of-mouth advertising has replaced magazines for this businessman.

## PUBLICITY/PROMOTIONAL ACTIVITIES

"Publicity is expensive, but the Japanese public likes it," said André Pachon in reference to the articles written about him, or rave reviews on his gourmet cuisine. Another entrepreneur, Chuck Wilson, fitness expert, agrees that his success on Japanese television, his movie appearances, and sales of his health/fitness books have definitely boosted membership in the health club of which he is managing partner. "It's short-lived fame, but it's certainly helped my main business. The difficulty of ascertaining the effects of advertising makes me believe that it's necessary to create an awareness that you exist," he said.

Wilson is also a strong advocate of educational programs, particularly as his field of health and fitness is relatively new and still developing in Japan. "Chronic smokers and drinkers abound here, and you have to have that educational process as part of a promotional campaign. Creating an awareness of health and fitness takes time, but you get a reasonable increase in sales. Convincing corporations, for example, to have health club memberships for employees is a new concept, but I use traditional appeals to preservation of human resources, the employees."

John McDowell, a New Zealander, is attempting to build a demand for his country's fruit juices and wines, and he believes that New Zealand enjoys a good reputation in Japan due to its appealing scenery and its image as a country catering to "things natural." He has thus marketed his products as those of New Zealand, rather than emphasizing the manufacturer, Barker's Company. "The quality and natural image are important, and to maintain that we have worked with the New Zealand Embassy to give the products the official sanction, even using a brass band from home to promote the products as New Zealand-based, not Barker's-based."

Another New Zealander, Hugh Kininmonth, has also played upon that image to sell sheepskin baby rugs and woolens. The problem, according to Kininmonth, is that Japanese may never have heard of the product and are suspicious. To educate Japanese consumers, promotional literature from New Zealand manufacturers is a must, and it has to be translated. Selling the items requires an extensive educational process, and the hand-in-hand cooperation of suppliers, which Kininmonth found hard to obtain, finding it easier to sell plain woolen yarn for knitting rather than woolen fashions, sheepskin rugs, or car seat covers that require adaptation to the market.

Walt Spillum of Danco Japan, Ltd. even borrowed money to have promotional literature translated, a must in Japan for consumer education, since the Japanese consumer's decision-making process from the point of the initial sales pitch to the consummation of the deal is quite lengthy, as compared to the U.S., and promotional materials can aid in speeding things up. (There are even various types of financing available from the Japanese government that are strictly to be used for promotional materials, translation, etc., although foreign entrepreneurs may not always have easy access to these.)

Terrie Lloyd of Linc Japan related how an "advance publicity" strategy could help foreigners with their sights on doing business in Japan. An Australian client sold articles and photos to a Japanese magazine while Lloyd's firm did the translations. This developed an image for the person in Japan that could be capitalized upon at a later date. Lloyd also added that a press release, if written properly, can often be an effective publicity tool, provided that someone working at the paper is your ally and puts it in the editor's box to get past the screening process. Attaching pictures to the release is also helpful.

Some entrepreneurs use promotional materials that are more subtle. Bunny Cramer's Witan Associates publishes a newsletter for clients to keep them abreast of corporate communications developments. Walt Spillum has formed a club for all purchasers of Lindal cedar homes, with members receiving a newsletter and having the option to attend meetings to get to know other homeowners in Japan and abroad. "It's a family orientation that is well-suited to the Japanese, who like exclusivity, group togetherness, and club activities."

When new concepts or products are involved, educational seminars for the wholesale trade, newsletters on updates, and detailed literature for the public (translated into Japanese), are all musts, according to the interviewed.

### DIRECT MARKETING/BULK MAIL RATES

Direct marketing, or selling directly to consumers by using the mails, represents under 1% of the retail sales market in Japan, but is expected to grow to around 30% by the year 2000, according to statistics compiled by Infoplan Japan, a market research firm. (The Japan Direct Marketing Association estimates, however, that the share will increase to only 12%.) The potential profits involved in the successful penetration of the complex Japanese distribution system make direct marketing an exciting alternative route for new businesses in Japan, yet Kerry Kennedy of Direct Marketing Services Japan, a direct market research firm, stated that, "There isn't the same creative talent or experience base or catalog/DM techniques here as in the U.S., for example, so Japan is like a newly industrialized country in the DM area."

The ACCJ has maintained that bulk mail rates for direct

marketing did not even exist until recently, but that due to the ACCJ's and Japan Direct Marketing Association's joint efforts, bulk mail rates were established. A directive was finally issued by the government that discounted regular first-class postage from October 1, 1987, as much as 30% for bulk mail but the discount applied only to first- and second-class mail, which does not include catalogs. Thus many businesses now are mailing promotional material from Hong Kong, which has bulk mail rates, a method that is still cheaper than mailing directly in Japan. (Kennedy did mention, however, that doing so is illegal, and if the Post Office intercepts the mailing, they will "dump it.")

Another DM-related problem is that of obtaining and maintaining customer mailing lists. (One entrepreneur stated that for those without money, using friends with access to such lists of consumers is one way to get around the problem.) Furthermore, one name can cost about ¥10, but if a new list is compiled, the cost can skyrocket to as much as ¥300 per name. As for toll-free numbers that assist direct marketing efforts, the system in Japan, unlike the U.S., restrains telemarketing as charges for calls are merely accepted by the business being contacted. Thus, each call is billed at the applicable long-distance rate, not uniformly as in the toll free "800" number system in the U.S., a costly proposition for small foreign businesses.

In 1985, net sales from DM were ¥830 billion, and in 1986, an Economic Planning Agency survey noted that 30% of the 1,485 respondents had made a purchase through the mails within the past year and 82% were satisfied. An article in the *Japan Times* by Laurel Miller recently noted that there are fewer complaints reported to the Ministry of International Trade and Industry's Consumer Protection Division for products purchased through the DM route, since consumers decide at home, alone, without high-pressure salesmen breathing down their necks. Since consumers don't have to fight crowds at department stores, can pay upon delivery, use credit cards, and are not charged for returns, DM is looking more and more attractive all the time to the Japanese housewife pressed for time. The best thing about DM, however, is that it allows businesses, large and small, to escape the complexities and frustrations inherent in the Japanese distribution system and the expense of establishing retail outlets. Direct marketing has special appeal for small businesses since mailings can be confined to geographical areas so that results are accountable, measurable and cost-effective, all important considerations for start-up ventures.

Two entrepreneurs in the advertising business had different opinions about direct marketing. Terrie Lloyd of Linc Japan said that many businesses were not brave enough yet to use DM, since they believe that it will "turn the Japanese off" to their products. However, Claus Regge of Network, Inc., a technical advertising firm, said that his company does direct mail campaigns every two to three years to solicit European business in Japan, using EC membership lists of companies engaged in technical businesses, and is happy with the results to date.

## SALES PROMOTION

Japan's Fair Trade Commission (JFTC) does not like promotion. That is, restrictions on premiums or sales incentives for consumers or the trade are very much in force, although outdated, and they are a source of trade friction between the U.S., France, Britain, and Japan.

The value of the giveaways attached to a product must be within 10% of the main product's price, and sales incentives, such as free trips for retailers if a large amount of products is sold over a given campaign period, are illegal. Foreign companies can't grab consumer attention with devices like rebates, coupons, sweepstakes, or premiums, and so foreign products become "high-priced specialty items" because market share is hard to capture.

The ACCJ's official position on this "premiums and promotions" issue is that in order for American business to have better access to the Japanese market, the JFTC should:

1. Reevaluate and adjust prize limits on sweepstakes, premiums, rebates, free samples, and giveaways;
2. Permit the publication of discount coupons in commercial periodicals in Japan;
3. Relax the JFTC regulations to allow all products to compete freely through sales promotions;
4. Consider abolishing all restrictions on premiums except those imposed under the Antimonopoly Act.

Oddly enough, the JFTC, while trying to stop unfair inducements to customers, is itself violating the antitrust laws by sponsoring groups that agree to limit sales promotions on a voluntary basis.

**TYPESETTING/PRINTING**

When the cheapest printing job in Japan for a 4-color, 2-page brochure is ¥50,000 more than the most expensive quote for the same job in Hong Kong, one can understand why many small businesses and advertising agencies have printing and typesetting done in Hong Kong. Even though money must be spent on a plane ticket in order to establish contacts with quality printers and perhaps even a 10% liaison commission must be paid to a Hong Kong businessman to set up and supervise the work, it is still cheaper to have color work printed in Hong Kong. (Black-and-white work can be more economically printed in Japan than in Hong Kong, however, provided that a provincial, non-Tokyo printer is used.)

There are three price ranges for printing/typesetting services in Japan: the Tokyo standard, the Japanese countryside standard (as in Fukushima), and the Hong Kong standard. However, the countryside printer is still more expensive by far than Hong Kong outfits, according to several experienced foreign entrepreneurs. (Of course, this problem has been exacerbated by the yen's currently high valuation, making out-of-country printing even more attractive.) As one ad agency owner noted, "Japanese printers, no matter what, just can't compete with Hong Kong." Even large printing companies, like Toppan, have branches in Hong Kong because it's substantially cheaper to have the work done there and sent back to Japan than to do it in Japan in the first place.

To emphasize the disparity in printing prices, the following is a 1987 comparative survey of the prices for 1,000 copies of a leaflet that uses four colors on one side, three colors on the other, and two transparencies (figures courtesy of Terrie Lloyd of Linc Japan):

| Printer Location | Estimate |
|---|---|
| Australia | ¥ 170,000 |
| Taiwan | ¥ 117,000 |
| Hong Kong (lowest price) | ¥ 77,000 |
| Hong Kong (highest price) | ¥ 100,000 |
| Japan (countryside) | ¥ 120,000 |
| Japan (Tokyo) | ¥ 200,000 |
| Japan (Tokyo; design studio) | ¥ 340,000 |

**Note:** If printing in Hong Kong, an additional ¥10,000 must be added for postage/shipping costs.

According to Claus Regge of Network, Inc., a technical advertising firm, the time factor is often a constraint on printing in Hong Kong. Therefore, for those in a real hurry, Regge offers a full menu of printing services, ranging from graphic design and typesetting, to hardware and software packages that allow a business to do its own in-house printing/typesetting. Since each job has differing requirements, Regge said that no price could be quoted offhand for any given assignment.

# 10

# Pros & Cons of Being
# a Foreign Business

The business people interviewed for this book have found many
sides to conducting business in Tokyo. Among the not-so-good
aspects are non-tariff barriers, or NTBs—cultural impasses not easily remedied by legislation, but which may be overcome by cultivating the qualities mentioned at the beginning of this book: optimism,
perseverance, and adaptation.

On the positive side, advantages are often present in being foreign and in business, albeit small business; for while small in Japan
is not necessarily beautiful, 99% of all enterprises in Japan are small-
and medium-sized, and account for 70% of all output, 62% of gross
wholesale sales, 79% of retail sales, and employ 81% of the work
force.

The following are some case histories of men and women doing
business in Japan.

## 1. Richard Bliah: Architect, Not Foreigner
French architect/designer Richard Bliah's most interesting observation was that he would not want to take advantage of being foreign in his business dealings because it would contradict his
professional policy announced to his employees that, "When you
work for me, you work for an architect, not a foreigner." As to
his customers, he knows that a certain amount of curiosity exists
because he is a foreigner, but since all of his business negotiations
are conducted in Japanese, he disregards it and proceeds à la
Japonaise.

Bliah stated positively that opportunity abounds in Japan,
particularly for those with confidence in their abilities and who have

specialized products or services to offer. He disagreed with the concept of pervasive NTBs and cultural friction, realizing that there are some difficulties, but by working with the Japanese Customs personnel, for example, interpersonal contact seemed to dispel the problems. "You must bring problems away from the papers and documents," he said. By dealing with problems on a one-to-one basis, but according to Japanese rules and regulations, you can satisfy the requirements *and* get things done. (In the future, though, Bliah would like to see the troublesome official procedures streamlined.)

Working with the Japanese has proved to him that being foreign is not the problem. "The problem is that we, as foreign companies, must be more patient. A government cannot change people's minds overnight," the architect stressed.

In his early years, Bliah worked for a Japanese company in Algeria, and eventually quit, feeling that the company's inability to allow him to independently negotiate with the Algerians in French—he was constantly reporting back to the company and being advised on how to proceed—evidenced a lack of confidence in his professional abilities. He learned that making an idea appear to be that of the Japanese, although it was his, was one way to achieve his goals; but since he felt little responsibility was being allotted to him, he decided to be in control of his own operation while using his adaptation to Japanese practices as a guide. S.E.C. K.K., his own company, was formed only 11 years ago, but with annual billings of ¥300 million, Bliah's growing pains have obviously paid off.

## 2. Bunny Cramer: Six of One, a Half Dozen of the Other

Bunny Cramer of Witan Associates felt that being foreign was positive to the point of being a necessity for her line of work (formulation of corporate communications materials), because native English speaking, reading, and writing skills are required. As to selling products, though, Ms. Cramer felt that there was no credit given for being foreign. "It all depends on what line of business you're in as to whether 'foreign' is good or bad," she said.

Her stories about leasing a copy machine and getting financing, which have been detailed in previous sections, do provide food for thought, however, about whether being foreign is a plus, at least in those spheres of activity.

### 3. Michael Dunn: Getting Away With It

According to Michael Dunn, an art/antique dealer, a foreign salesman can usually demand entrance and get away with more than a Japanese who is trying to sell something. "You can get away with more than you deserve, though that's changed somewhat in the past few years." He also believes that Japan is an easy country to do business in because a high ethical standard is present. "It is a bit like England—done on a handshake. Just on trust alone, I have several million yen in inventory."

On the other hand, he quickly related his encounters with the classic NTB, the Japanese Customs procedures, which he stumbled into when importing and exporting fine art. He concluded, "If I can't carry it, I don't ship it. The Japanese bureaucracy defies logic in a way no other civilization's does. So don't deal with it if at all possible," adding that exports of Japanese art must often have government permission.

Dunn did readily admit that if papers are filed correctly the first time, down to the dotted "i," customs problems can often be avoided. However, he also told a tale that seemed to contradict that conclusion. A friend wanted to reimport a pure gold Japanese screen, but the screen was classified as bullion. Since a bullion dealer's license was needed, and only Japanese may obtain such a license, the transaction was denied clearance. "To solve some problems, if you threaten to expose them internationally and call in the press, actions change sometimes," he says.

### 4. Fran Kuzui: I Am Foreign

Fran Kuzui of Kuzui Enterprises stressed that when in Japan, she maintains her American identity and does not play a Japanese role as many foreign business people are inclined to do. "I don't say 'san' when addressing people, as it makes me uncomfortable. I'm foreign, not Japanese, and I don't believe that 'foreignness' has hurt me when I participate in business here," she says. Other business owners have concurred, saying that to "out-Japanese" the Japanese doesn't work and that bowing deeper won't help you, and, in fact, may hurt you.

Kuzui has retained her American manner of clinching a business deal by requiring a bottom line signature to seal commitment, unlike the Japanese "gentlemen's agreement" way of doing business. Says Kuzui, "If they don't want to sign, I know they're not really interested. It's a symbol, not a legal entanglement, because for small-scale projects, it's not worth it to sue." Other entrepreneurs agreed that "handshake" deals were rare and commitment on paper was a necessity, if only a symbolic one.

While she and her Japanese husband work together to smooth out frictions between the Japanese and U.S. parties to contracts in the film and entertainment industry, providing a buffer zone/liaison to both sides, she said that because Japanese companies don't want to deal with Americans if they can deal with a fellow countryman, her role in negotiations in Japan is more covert than in the U.S. Kuzui felt that she would never consider doing business without a Japanese partner, because the cultural link is vital to understanding what is really happening in business deals, since it's not always visible on the surface.

Her biggest revelation concerned the mixing of business and friendship. After spending money on Japanese clients, personally catering to them and considering them as more than mere business associates, she was surprised to find how coolly they reacted. "I realized that it's not personal. It's company versus company, and this is how the Japanese behave with each other anyway." She found it hard to accept, since in America business and friendship are often interchangeable.

### 5. Chuck Wilson: The Personal Touch

According to Chuck Wilson, communicating to the Japanese that you have a product that can be identified or related to their culture, and that you have personal ability, are absolute essentials. "If the concept works from a *Japanese* standpoint, your problems are minimized. Once you get past the basic problems of a difficult distribution system and the language, you then have to see the personalized nature of Japanese business and how you and your product fit in that scheme." Wilson reiterated that if the Japanese do not need your product, you have to ensure that they *do,* creating a need in line with their cultural values.

Because Wilson provides a service (health and physical fitness consulting and fitness centers), he finds that the Japanese are very cautious and conservative about paying for something intangible. However, by working personally with clients, and becoming an integral part of their daily regimen, he convinced them by example of the benefits of health and fitness. "Use personal assurances repeatedly. Respect for you and liking you as a person are two different things in Japan," Wilson cautions.

### 6. Reiko Lyster: Three Strikes, But Never Out

Reiko Lyster of Elle International has encountered customs problems in her business, the import and sale of fine French cosmetics. The Ministry of Health and Welfare *(Kōseishō)* regulations have also caused constant interference. "They are trying to simplify, but they drag their feet," she sighs. She also noted that marketing expenses and a complex distribution system push product prices up for foreign-made goods, but since foreign goods can compete with Japanese products as to innovation and quality, she believes that foreign items are not really expensive in comparison to domestic brands, as is often charged.

Strikes two and three, being foreign and being a woman, have hindered her. Even though she was born a Japanese citizen, she acquired American citizenship after marriage with an American and is therefore regarded as a foreigner. Ms. Lyster noted that as long as she confines herself to just cosmetics and beauty items, the retailers and dealers tend to forget about her gender and nationality, and at times, she admitted, it even seemed to help her to be different. However, she also believes that banks and department store managers do not understand her motivations, or why a woman would want to be CEO of her own company. "Maybe it's her husband's business or she's helping him out, they think. I'm not taken too seriously. Even my Japanese male friends who are entrepreneurs can't believe I'm in business with more than 120 employees and that I do it alone."

On the reverse side, by getting people's attention because of her unique traits, once the barriers were broken, being different put her in a better position, although she was still not accepted completely by any means. She believes that her ability to be feminine and still be a tough businesswoman makes a good and lasting impression, though her final word of caution is that women are not respected in Japan as in the West, and that there is a long road ahead before that day arrives.

### 7. Neil Butler: Three Little Words

Australian Neil Butler, importer of eucalyptus oil and computers, thinks there are both positive and negative aspects to being foreign, but threw out three essentials that he believes are mandatory for business people in Japan. "A normal Japanese wouldn't have made the same contacts I've made due to my 'foreignness.' You need connections, time, and effort, though, in this market, particularly because the Japanese are not especially international."

## 8. Hugh Kininmonth: It's Us, Not Them

Hugh Kininmonth, a New Zealander, thinks that his problems stem from the New Zealand side, not the Japanese end. He reports that New Zealand companies think that the Japanese market is full of problems and is too expensive, and they don't want to get involved. Since some small companies in the land of kiwis had had trouble with Japanese agents, they did not want to get committed to the market again. Thus, even though Kininmonth had offered to buy directly from the companies, rather than just represent them, the traders were all reluctant. "Only one company will supply custom-orders to suit Japanese tastes (which is another problem), or supply brochures for promotional purposes," he complained.

In Japan, a very competitive spirit, the need for contacts in strategic locations, such as department stores, and language ability all are musts, believes Kininmonth, but added that lack of language doesn't hinder some people, citing the example of a friend who had conquered the market despite his handicap.

"It helps to be foreign 80% of the time; the other 20% of the time, it doesn't." Kininmonth strongly asserts that you must ascertain your position in Japanese society, a difficult assessment, and then act your role: not too superior, not too inferior, but not ever really equal.

## 9. Niels Martenson: Import Impasse

Niels Martenson, a German entrepreneur who represents various foreign products, listed the mandatory customs quota system for some items, like aluminum containers, as troublesome. Along with the brokerage system for customs clearance, which drives costs up and is not within the direct control of the importer, a longer time is needed for clearance in Japan and high fees must be paid to brokers. Having a quota system means that duty is not levied until the quota is filled, but as he pointed out, it usually only takes two to three months to fill the quota. The quotas protect certain industries, like the aluminum industry, which cannot compete with cheaper imports from the developing nations. The problem of overcoming the substandard image accompaying products from developing nations is a further concern.

On dealing with the Japanese, he says, "Some people like you just because you're foreign; others don't for that same reason. However, I don't let that bother me; I just avoid those types."

### 10. Claus Regge: The Good Life

Another German, Claus Regge, feels that NTBs are a problem blown out of proportion, and that contrary to opinion and popular sentiment, products are not necessarily more difficult to sell in Japan than services. He explains that Customs has helped him by bending over backward to clear his imported items, even completing the unfinished documentation upon arrival from Europe. "You can't strong-arm the government here. Whenever they're in doubt, I've always paid lower duties, but I know that putting merchandise in the right category is important. I learned by trial and error." He related the story of separating oboes and their cases when shipping as higher duties are levied when shipped together.

Regge also believes it is easier to meet people on a first-time basis if you are a non-Japanese, as certain privileges are enjoyed: namely, the Japanese accept your expertise on areas outside of Japan. As a bonus, it is also not necessary for foreigners to socialize to the degree that Japanese do in order to build business contacts because it is accepted that you have different priorities.

### 11. Dave Wouters: The Value-Added Approach

Dave Wouters of Wouters & Associates experienced many problems dealing with Customs, unlike Claus Regge, when he was trying to import freeze-dried coffee and fruits. So many problems were encountered, in fact, that he gave up importing. "The coffee remained in a warehouse until they (the Ministry of Health and Welfare) could determine the process of freeze-drying the coffee, and I never could get approval on the fruit. Providing services goes smoother, however, where I deal with foreign business, and there are no barriers or discriminatory practices." Wouters felt that there were relatively few trade barriers in the service sector, as opposed to the manufactured goods area.

Wouters elaborated on the "value-added" dilemma, or the need to be Japanese in addition to offering the right item at the right price. He recounted the story of representing Exide battery company in Japan, stating that even though his product was cheaper and of a better quality than that of the Japanese manufacturers, the buyers told him point blank that they wanted to buy Japanese. "Forget equal market access because aside from the normal considerations of quality, price, delivery and service, you must be Japanese."

Conversely, Wouters believed that if one is tough and continues to push for success in this market, achievement is possible, a sentiment expressed by most of the entrepreneurs. The need for commitment and patience plus flexibility are the keynotes. In another businessman's words, "The tail often wags the dog," meaning that changing direction at the appropriate time, and progressing from one's original plans to a final form quite different in scope, are necessary actions for success in Japan.

## 12. The Parallel Import Specter

A businessman importing high-quality pet food said that his main objection to business practices in Japan concerned the policy of the Japanese government to allow parallel imports, thereby neglecting the hard work and efforts of businesses that develop the markets first. "It's a free ride for those coming after I've advertised and developed the market," he stated. Eleven years after starting his business, he employs 45 workers, has numerous distributorships, and annual sales of ¥1 billion, revealing a man who has pioneered the development of the top-flight pet food market.

This gentleman well understood the problem of undercutting, as he worked for a major electronics company in Japan developing a distribution system for their products for nine years, and after doing so, was informed that the company had learned adequately from him and that his services were no longer required.

### 13. Graham Pike: The Old-Boy Network

"If a foreigner is here long enough, the Japanese seem to feel sympathetic and find some work for you," said Graham Pike of Pacific Marine, Ltd., a shipping company. Pike also believes that foreigners are not required to pay as high a price as the Japanese when it comes to socializing for cultivation of contacts. However, he doubts that being foreign bestows any particular advantages now, due to the information explosion. "Many Japanese now know what only a foreigner used to know because of gradual internationalization."

He feels that the Japanese enjoy doing business with him because "it tickles their vanity." Recalling that although the Japanese like to come to his home for dinner meetings, and offer him jobs in order to impress their friends with the fact that they are dealing with a foreigner, on balance, Pike did not see any distinction between the "old-boy network" in England and the Japanese way of doing business which stresses contacts and ties.

### 14. Valerie Gaynard: No Need For *Nihongo*

While many entrepreneurs believed that language skills were a top priority, several had little or no Japanese-language ability, relying instead on right-hand assistants or translators, and yet, were very successful. Valerie Gaynard of Interior Decor, Ltd. stated that she used translators in business negotiations with her Japanese clients and was turning a profit of over $40,000 (U.S.) per month in 1986, so language does not appear to be a hindrance in her case. Being a foreign woman with a get-up-and-go type of aggressiveness seems to have helped Ms. Gaynard get where she is today, contrary to the stereotypical views that such women are out of place in Japan.

### 15. Thomas Caldwell: The Adaptation Allergy

Thomas Caldwell of Caldwell & Associates feels that his problems lie mostly with U.S. exporters unwilling to modify products for the Japanese market, not with the Japanese. He detailed the story of a Japanese hotel that wanted 80 custom-made bar counters but the U.S. concern would not change the height or the color to meet Japanese requests.

Caldwell feels foreigners have been given too much latitude in Japan and that Americans overseas are afraid of selling in Japan due to the myth that only a big company can survive. He advises that participation in trade shows, personal involvement with customers, continual follow-ups on contacts, and taking Japanese-language study seriously enable many foreign businessmen to be successful.

Lastly, and most importantly, Caldwell firmly believes that working together with small Japanese companies is the best way to succeed, because the small company is more open-minded and easier to deal with. As for rules and procedures and always following the official line, "We are guests here, and problems can be overcome with timing and the help of the Japanese people, who I believe are basically interested in helping foreigners in Japan."

### 16. Jeanne Goldberszt: Comme Ci, Comme Ça

Madame Jeanne Goldberszt of Style France, importers of French interior decorations and furnishings, sums up the situation on foreigners in business in Japan when she says, "Good points about being foreign and in business in Japan? It's very hard to answer, but when I see the troubles my Japanese customers have, I think mine aren't any worse. It's difficult for everybody in business here."

# 11

# Business Advice

The following is a list of the dos and don'ts of doing business in Japan from the voices of experience, the entrepreneurs themselves. If there seem to be contradictions in certain places, remember that in Japan, as in philosophy, there are no real contradictions, only conflicting premises. "Conflicting premises" in the case of the foreign business people in Japan can be translated as "differing circumstances." Thus, although not everything applies to every business owner, here are some words of wisdom that may be useful to aspiring entrepreneurs:

| DO | DON'T |
|---|---|
| 1. Check your marketing strategy and do it yourself. | 1. Don't depend on others for market research or education about Japan or for translations. |
| 2. Make a niche in the very competitive Japanese market by finding a unique product/service. | 2. Don't go into import; export is better. |
| 3. Sell ONLY high-quality products. | 3. Don't show "soft spots," your lack of financial wherewithal, or that you are small in scale; small is not a plus in Japan for the foreign business. |

4. Trademark your products first to avoid problems later.

4. Don't go into business alone; have a Japanese partner or spouse with you all the way for language assistance and business financing aid.

5. Learn Japanese by all means. (Qualification: several of the entrepreneurs didn't know or use Japanese, yet were quite successful as they were dealing with mostly foreign customers/ suppliers, or had top-notch bilingual assistants. However, most advised learning the language.)

5. Don't rely on Japanese staff for translations: check it yourself.

6. Finance yourself—see what you need by making an estimate, THEN DOUBLE IT. (Due to hidden costs and lengthy payment systems, you need capital to tide you over for one year at least.)

6. Don't come to Japan to get rich quick: plan to be here for a while. This is not a get-in-and-get-out-quick market.

7. Do get a full-time sales-man, as face-to-face business contacts are a must.

7. Don't cold call.

8. Be in touch with suppliers and clients: get a facsimile machine (fax) and a telex.

8. Don't deal with Japanese mid-level managers; deal directly with Japanese suppliers, as the former do not have the authority to make decisions in all cases.

9. Have a secure supplier who is 100% behind you—and will supply samples, promotional materials, financial aid.

9. If you can't find reliable suppliers abroad, don't get into business in Japan, as consistency and reliability are musts.

10. Join self-help groups like small business organizations for contacts and information.

10. Don't hesitate to ask for help here; someone will know more than you and be willing to share.

11. Do get to know people in the system as Time = Contacts = Good Business.

11. Don't forget to constantly follow-up on sales/service personally; that extra service is especially important in Japan.

12. Know the system of payments and also that it takes 3–5 years to show a profit.

12. Don't be impatient and don't invest in fixed assets, space, or equipment if you can help it.

13. Do have the conviction and commitment to be in Japan.

13. Don't come to Japan unless you are prepared to invest your time and effort.

14. Be prepared: expect obstacles and headaches and a longer time to accomplish things. Understand the slower sales process and time needed to build customer relations.

14. Don't ever give up; be positive.

15. Be willing to adapt products to the market.

15. Don't pursue sales as you would in your home country; it may look like the West, but it isn't.

16. Know whom you're dealing with or getting into business with; beware of unsavory investors.

17. Go to Japanese trade shows, set up booths, and have *meishi*: be there in person.

18. Incorporate a *kabushiki kaisha* or *yūgen-gaisha* for Japanese presence; a trade-mission type of appearance isn't enough for the long term.

In addition, three businesswomen gave advice that you may wish to ponder. Their three maxims were:

1. Use your foreign nationality to positive advantage.
2. Unless there is a real desire to be in Japan, or unless there is a specific reason for being here (e.g., marriage with a

Japanese), your motivations must be strong, and sound reasons must exist for being in business; no illusions about business opportunities or success in Japan will do.

3. Think it over several times when starting a business, as returns are low, it takes hard work and capital, and profits don't show up until several years later; if immediate money is your object, it is better to invest abroad and not to be in Japan in business.

# 12

# Business Organizations

Many foreign small business owners in Japan (two-thirds of those interviewed to be exact), belong to a small business organization. Whether part of a chamber of commerce, a formal association, or an informal gathering, small business organizations have brought together members who share common goals, experiences, frustrations, and a need to be informed about various aspects of doing business in Japan.

Of the organizations currently in existence, the American Chamber of Commerce's Small Business Promotion Committee has the longest history, dating from about 1980. The Australian Business Association and the Business Owner's Club were founded in 1985. Thus, organizations for the promotion of small business in Japan are a relatively new phenomenon, and give proof of an ever-increasing number of foreigners becoming involved in business in Japan. An examination of some organizations follows.

## THE FRENCH CONNECTION: BUSINESS OWNER'S CLUB IN JAPAN

Frenchman Richard Bliah, an architect/designer, prides himself on having built his very first house, a UFO-type structure, in the backyard of his professor's home in Japan. He can also be proud of having started the Business Owner's Club in Japan, an organization formed to aid European entrepreneurs. The Club was inaugurated at the beginning of 1985, has about 20 members, and is affiliated with the French Chamber of Commerce.

According to Bliah, the French Chamber has three types of members: large companies, expatriates working for the former, and a few independent businessmen. Since the emphasis at the Chamber is on the first two groups, the Club was formed to provide the extras that the Chamber did not offer to them, that is, self-help, support, information directed specifically to small businesses, and fraternity. "We must fight to make our own way here without head office support. By doing so and making this group, we may stimulate other people to start up in Japan on their own," Bliah says.

This group is a self-help group for the sharing of problems, goals, and information, being specifically oriented to the small business by offering practical information, rather than focusing on political issues. Regular monthly meetings are held and there is a yearly membership fee of ¥30,000. Since the group is still relatively new, there are no seminars or educational programs yet.

While the Club is small, and collectively, the members' sales/billings do not equal even one large French company's yearly sales, its formation is not related to the question of volume of sales, but to cultural exchange, the arrangement of trade balances with Japan, and (the originally French word) entrepreneurship. "The Japanese government should encourage the small foreign businesses to be here because they add to economic and cultural exchange." Unfortunately, immigration is a continuing problem, as visas may be curtailed suddenly in business midstream, according to Bliah, and a businessman could theoretically be requested to leave within 24 hours if the slightest trouble occurs, all of which leaves business planning and development on uncertain ground and gives the entrepreneur a generally uneasy feeling. "Since in Japan you must have something to bring to the culture that Japanese themselves don't provide, another problem exists of being allowed to stay for only very short periods, three to six months even, to provide a service, and then you are forced to leave." Bliah did finish by saying that since six or seven years ago the situation has changed somewhat, particularly with the move of the immigration office to the headquarters at Otemachi (a prime business district), which is more spacious and seemingly symbolic of the government's good intentions to change its policy.

Aside from visas, the habitual problem of dealing with banks is a major concern for the Club, and the availability of low-interest loans is the dream of many of the members. "Foreign banks only accomodate big business, and Japanese banks need time to build ties, time that we don't have. We want to ask these Japanese banks to invest in us."

Bliah also wants to publicize the group to other chambers of commerce, and indeed has become a supporting associate of the ACCJ, along with Japanese government organs like MITI, the MOF, etc., and through these various groups, works to solve problems. Groups aside, Bliah says, "We're individual members of the Chamber and [we] follow the spirit of it, but the group has special motivations and very human-level problems. We're business owners; [we're] not defending concerns of a company that isn't ours. So, ultimately, our interests are not the same as [those of] other Chamber members."

Visions for the individual members and the Club are large in scale, and it is hoped that the Club can publicize constructive criticism of Japan abroad to help Europeans understand the Japanese and Japan's business environment. "After all, we love it here and plan to be here, and it's good for the Japanese people as well." Also in the works is an ambitious project to purchase land and have Bliah design an office building to house these European businessmen in order to get reduced office rents.

"Small companies have deep roots, wide experience, and continuing human contact, so their contributions can be very important," said Bliah. The Business Owner's Club is primarily a group of entrepreneurs using their collective experiences in Japan to effect cultural change, and change in the business world of Japan as well.

The Business Owner's Club of Japan
201 Shibuya Homes, 2-1 Udagawa-cho
Shibuya-ku, Tokyo 150
Tel: (03) 477-7488
Telex: J 32460AUDIODSN

## THE AUSTRALIAN BUSINESS ASSOCIATION

In 1985, Neil Butler, Viv Duus, and Roger March decided that the time was ripe for the formation of an Australian business association. A growing number of Australians were in business in Japan due to the working-holiday visa program, which allows Australians to come to Japan for six to eighteen months and work in order to promote cultural exchange. This presence prompted Butler to research the viability of forming a group for information exchange, support, and learning how to solve visa problems after the working-holiday period expired.

The ABA was started in June of 1985 to serve those interests and currently has about 65 members. The activities of its members range from market research, trade, and translation services, to entertainment promotion and film production. Since 1,315 Australians and New Zealanders visited Japan on the working-holiday visa between 1981 and 1985, the mailing list and types of activities of ABA's membership are expanding accordingly. Fortunately, the Australians consider variety and volume a strong point of their organization, not a divisive force.

Former president Viv Duus, now resident in Australia, stated that Australians are a relatively small group in Japan, as compared to Americans, which means that Australian businessmen can get an audience with government officials fairly easily. "Our group has clout because it's easier for us to get access to officials (than for Americans). We've already met with cabinet ministers on a visit to Japan, though the people only had about 40 minutes to mingle with Australian businessmen. We also get more backing because Australia is out to expand exports," noted Duus. ABA's goals of creating a higher profile for small Australian business, meeting governmental officials, both Japanese and Australian, and solving visa problems certainly seem obtainable with these types of activities on the agenda.

The consensus of the ABA directors at this writing is that preserving the group as a separate entity from the Chamber is essential. Reminiscent of the French business owners' situation, the Australians feel that the Chamber focuses mostly on larger concerns, so there is often a lack of common interests. "The big Australian companies don't even give us work here," said one entrepreneur, a similar complaint of other foreign small businesses interested in working with larger counterparts from their home countries that are already established in Japan.

To ABA members, the independence of their group is more than a representation of their individualism, it represents a practical, self-help network that had not previously existed, and the establishment of an information network is actually the most important aspect of the ABA, rather than political representation. Thus, the Chamber's and ABA's functions are distinguishable.

According to Chris Hodgens and Roger March, founding members, relations between the ACCJ, the ABA, and the Australian embassy are so good that the three groups hope to set up regular three-way meetings, and have already laid the groundwork for this. Cooperation, rather than competitiveness, seems to be the hallmark of the ABA/ACCJ/embassy relationship, each recognizing their respective abilities and the roles of Australians in business in Japan.

The ABA has a formal set of rules outlining aims, membership categories, Executive Committee functions, meeting formalities, dues, etc. The ABA meets a minimum of six times a year, and distributes a monthly newsletter jampacked with information to keep members informed of upcoming events, seminars, meetings, business opportunities in Japan and Australia, and current events back home. Workshops on taxation, incorporation of a company, and computer automation are examples of the practical information that ABA programs disseminate and that members are looking for. A membership directory is also available.

The ABA has recently received the aid of JASI, Japan-Australia Systems International. They have contributed, free of charge, office space, a secretary, and a permanent phone line to coordinate ABA activities. The organization sees the ABA as a vitally important exchange link, since more and more Australians are working and living in Japan. More good news is that the Australian Trade Commission has also offered to provide information on the ABA and membership directories to visiting Australian businessmen as well as use of embassy facilities. The biggest bonus, though, is that the Commission has offered to set up contacts with small Japanese businesses.

The Zainichi Ōsutoraria Bijinesu Kyōkai (ABA's Japanese name) has particular aims, namely, to promote membership's interests in a variety of fields; to allow for members' exchange of information and resources; to promote Australia-Japan ties; to exchange resources and information with other groups approved by the ABA; and to cooperate with the latter where mutual interests are present.

The Australian Business Association in Japan
3-14-6 Ginza
Chuo-ku, Tokyo 104
Tel: (03) 5565-1361
Fax. (03) 545-8949

## THE SMALL BUSINESS PROMOTION COMMITTEE

In 1986, the American Chamber of Commerce in Japan's Small Business Promotion Committee debated its name, some members wishing to change it to the "Independent Business Committee." Since the Internal Affairs Committee of ACCJ refused to allow the name change, however, SBPC remains the Committee's name.

The 1985 Committee goals announced the need to broaden the appeal of the Committee to attract more members, and to change the name from the SBPC to a broader-based title to help achieve this. With an average luncheon attendance of under twenty people, the Committee felt a need to reveal itself to a wider audience, especially since it has been estimated that 1,000 Americans are operating independently in Japan.

However, there was a split between the members who wanted to attract owners and executives of larger businesses, and those who wished to help the truly "small," independent businessman.

Staffing, financial assistance, and the high costs of running a business in Japan are, of course, mandatory considerations for every foreign business. However, the interests of large businesses are not always the same as those of entrepreneurs who must assume personal liability, are unable to offer the enticement of working for a "name" firm, and lack attractive financial inducements. These shortcomings make hiring good Japanese personnel much more difficult for the small business owner who is "generic," or without a brand name. Moreover, the unavailability of financing for the small business from foreign and Japanese banks often forces the concern to use the entrepreneur's capital to invest and set up in Japan, a problem foreign executives of subsidiary operations with access to banking services do not face. High costs, likewise, must be dealt with alone, as there is no home office footing set-up bills or tiding over the business with start-up capital.

Concern had also been expressed about the image projected to the Japanese by the name "Small Business Committee," as some former members considered themselves anything but small in terms of sales/billings and staff employed, although on a relative scale the businesses were small. These larger businesses preferred using the word "independent," since even though most businesses in Japan are small, the connotations of a "mom and pop" enterprise were not exactly "prestigious." (However, when one looks at the Tokyo Chamber of Commerce's informational guide and other materials, which repeatedly stress "small and medium enterprise" financing, groups, etc., it becomes clear that to the Japanese Chamber of Commerce, small businesses are the backbone of the economy and need support, not disdain.)

Name considerations aside, the Committee battled for a few years to revise the dues structure of the ACCJ in order to make it more equitable. (Even though a sliding scale was employed to determine dues for company memberships, the dues structure was slanted toward big business.) Perhaps the new category of "non-voting individual" created in 1987 will attract new members, but at ¥80,000 per year it may still be too costly for small businesses when compared to other chambers and business organizations. (Compare the Tokyo Chamber of Commerce fees, given later on in this book.) As one SBPC member stated, "The benefits I get from the Chamber are many and the fees are worth it, but the payment of quarterly dues is burdensome."

As to those quarterly dues, all companies, large and small, must pay a ¥60,000 entrance fee, and the most inexpensive category for businesses is ¥140,000 per year, payable quarterly. The sliding scale used for companies is as follows: Category A: gross income less than ¥500 million pays annual dues of ¥140,000; Category B: ¥500 million or more but less than ¥2,000 million pays annual dues of ¥165,000; Category C: ¥2,000 million or more but less than ¥10,000 million pays annual dues of ¥190,000; and Category D: ¥10,000 million or more pays annual dues of ¥225,000. Since the price differential does not take into account companies with substantially smaller gross incomes, however, and the disparity between categories is not exceptionally large, the new non-voting individual category may possibly be attractive to proprietors.

The SBPC has concentrated on providing a forum for discussion of problems and information exchange, but particular emphasis has been placed on establishing financial aid for small businesses. To that end, Walt Spillum and Dick Adler, both business owners, formed a financial resource group to filter and disseminate information on financing available to small businesses. (Adler, as a former SBPC chairman, and Spillum were the first foreign small business owners to obtain government-assisted loans without a Japanese guarantor's signature and, in Adler's case, without collateral.) Spillum obtained his loan due to the all-out efforts of the SBPC, which influenced MITI to take action on his loan applications. "Without the backing of the ACCJ and this Committee, I know that getting the loan would have been nearly impossible," said Spillum. All Committee members have thus agreed that close relations with the Japanese government should be maintained and cultivated.

The Committee has also worked with the American embassy to obtain trade lists of potential representatives in Japan for U.S. exporters and cooperated with JETRO for trade shows and the promotion of American-manufactured items. A 1981 position paper by the Committee was used to make representations to the U.S. Congress about the needs of American small businesses in Japan.

Some trouble spots for the operational side of the Committee include the lack of programs and joint meetings catering specifically to small businesses. Furthermore, the Committee's membership base has not greatly expanded since its inception in 1981, its momentum being maintained solely by core members. Unfortunately, potential members balk at joining ACCJ because of the perception that the organization is basically for big business; few know that the SBPC exists to serve smaller concerns.

Some starts have been made to publicize the SBPC, to develop business financing information programs, and to set aside more time for regular luncheons to discuss problems. Most interestingly, the Committee passed a resolution in 1986 to encourage large ACCJ member corporations to do business with SBPC members when reasonably feasible, and where price and other relevant considerations are equal with the competition. As Wouters noted, this is the way that Japanese business has succeeded, by the large aiding the small. Larger American businesses in Japan, the SBPC felt, should be aware of the U.S. entrepreneurial presence in Japan and utilize their services/products. Helping each other to promote American interests in Japan is, after all, the ultimate goal of the Chamber and every member's indirect goal, despite fundamental differences of size and scope of operation.

At this writing, the Kansai chapter of the ACCJ, based in Osaka, is attempting to target small businesses for membership. Recognizing the growth of small businesses in Japan, the ACCJ seems to be launching a new policy of attracting small business owners as members.

The Small Business Promotion Committee
   of the American Chamber of Commerce in Japan
7th Floor, Fukide No. 2 Bldg, 4-1-21 Toranomon,
Minato-ku, Tokyo 105
Tel: (03) 433-5381

Kansai Chapter (Osaka): c/o Searle Yakuhin K.K.,
Osaka Nishi, P.O. Box 47, Osaka 550-91
Tel: (06) 541-3333
(Kansai Chapter includes Osaka, Kyoto, Kobe, Nagoya, Kure, and Hiroshima)

## THE INTERNATIONAL BUSINESS ASSOCIATION

The International Business Association was founded in 1985 by David Dvash, the associate publisher of the *Kyoto Journal*, a magazine on Japanese culture, because the small business owners in the cities of Osaka, Kyoto, and thereabouts, known as the Kansai area, all have to overcome the same types of problems. The most obvious and difficult obstacle according to 1987 president Sandy Taubenkimel is "how to penetrate the Japanese market," since new companies may not understand the workings of the Japanese system or have any information on it.

Taubenkimel is the owner of a management consulting company, Howard Roberts Associates, and has personally experienced the dilemmas of entering the market. He says that he can clearly recognize the problems because they are so commonplace and apply to all fields.

There are currently 30 members from about 10 different countries. Dues are ¥12,000 per year and the group meets once a month in an open-forum setting to discuss problem spots. From import/export and entering the market to understanding how to do business in Japan, the group covers all avenues in its meetings. While the Association has no aspirations in the political direction, it does work with various government agencies and the ACCJ in Osaka in order to get its members known and to get information for them.

Taubenkimel believes that the Kansai area is much more progressive than Tokyo and that Japanese firms in the Kansai area are truly interested in doing business overseas, and so the atmosphere is more open-minded than in Tokyo. According to him, foreign firms are and will be entering the Osaka area at a faster rate, evidencing the acceptance of them in the Kansai world of business.

## THE CANADIAN CHAMBER OF COMMERCE

The Chamber, founded in the early 1980s, counts as its members "individual Canadians active in business" in Japan. In a recently compiled membership list supplied by the Chamber, 20 individuals were identified as business entrepreneurs, out of the total individual membership of about 200 and company membership of 55.

The Chamber's main purpose is to promote Japan-Canada commercial relations, which includes learning about how to do business in Japan, finding solutions to problems, and introducing members to other Canadians in business, all three being necessary activities for those who run small businesses. The Chamber's business and associate business membership categories both cost ¥75,000 per year.

The following is a current list of some of the small businesses in the Chamber:

1. Import of cosmetics and textiles
2. Import and sale of home products
3. General engineering company
4. Market research company
5. Film and television production company
6. Translation services
7. Direct marketing services
8. Import of sporting goods
9. Travel and leisure promotion/advertising
10. Import of furs and petroleum products
11. Import of Canadian artworks and crafts
12. Investment consulting/corporate communications company
13. Symphony concert organization/music promotion company
14. Financial planning services
15. Advertising agency

Dan McVety, the Chamber's manager, reported that he receives a few calls every week from Canadian entrepreneurs wanting to set up shop who are either in Japan already or are in Canada and want to come to Japan. For example, one man is now out in the Japanese countryside looking for space to set up a mushroom factory. Another located in Canada wants to move to Japan to import and distribute "Canadian Rockies" mineral water, as he has tied up with Ajinomoto, a large food and spice company, for distribution purposes.

The biggest barriers to doing business in Japan, McVety said, are the registration procedures for small companies and visa problems. McVety was most encouraging as he announced the Chamber's willingness to aid entrepreneurs with the red tape and the legal requirements. "If you know the right people, and we do, you can get your visa," McVety stated. (Simplifying immigration procedures for businessmen and assisting more Canadians to enter the market are two of the major issues that the Chamber and its new director, Robert A. Fairweather, are attempting to tackle.)

The Canadian Chamber is geared to help entrepreneurs get through the initial stages of corporate set-up and visa requirements, leaving business, distribution, and sales to the entrepreneur. Of course, information on those activities is available at Chamber functions and seminars and in the *Chamber News,* a quarterly publication filled with notices, news, etc.

The Canadian Chamber of Commerce in Japan may be contacted through the Canadian embassy, Tel: (03) 447-9767.

## THE BRITISH CHAMBER OF COMMERCE

The British Chamber has no small business promotion committee as the ACCJ does, but since the total membership of the organization is much smaller (only about 200), seminars and programs can be offered that appeal to most members. Spokesman Ian DeStains observed that the American Chamber is so large, in comparison to the British Chamber, the Small Business Promotion Committee had to be created to fulfill the wishes of small business owners.

There are now 38 individual members, but not all of these are business owners, and many are people who do not belong to a major corporation.

One businessman, David Parry, noted that the entrepreneurial types are young British nationals or former expatriates who wish to remain in Japan after a company stint is over. He suggested that informal gatherings of particular categories of businessmen, such as English-language school owners, probably meet in local "pubs" to discuss issues.

At any rate, no formal organization exists to date for British nationals, but, as Parry said, "Maybe one needs to be started."

# 13

# Professional Clubs

There are several business and professional clubs that can provide not only useful information and networking contacts, but good camaraderie as well. Some of the recommended organizations include:

## 1. The KAISHA Society

Organized for foreigners working in Japanese companies, the KAISHA Society meets once a month to discuss such diverse topics as job responsibilities of foreign workers, benefits of working in Japan, conflict resolution, and negotiation styles of the Japanese. Members also give short presentations on Japanese companies or industries.

The philosophy of the Society is symbolized by its name, the word *kaisha* meaning company or firm. The basic tenets of the Society are:

| | |
|---|---|
| **K**nowledge | —understanding through experience |
| **A**ssociation | —joining with others to share experiences in order to gain new knowledge |
| **I**nsight | —the capacity to discern the true nature of an experience, through knowledge and association |
| **S**ynthesis | —the joining of individual insights into a coherent whole |
| **H**ope | —confidence, positive expectation |
| **A**ction | —working to achieve personal and professional growth by direct involvement |

For anyone working in Japan, entrepreneur or not, the information on business "Japan style" and foreign contacts within Japanese firms should certainly be of import.

The KAISHA Society
c/o The Press Club
Yurakucho Denki Bldg. 20th F.
1-7-1 Yurakucho
Chiyoda-ku, Tokyo 100
Tel: (03) 211-3161/7

2. SWET (Society of Writers, Editors and Translators)

This group counts among its members people involved in the above professions as well as teachers, researchers, rewriters, designers, and copywriters. They hold meetings and workshops five to six times a year and publish a monthly newsletter, and as of January 1987, the group had over 450 members.

The organization is primarily for those wishing to share experiences, information, and expertise involving English writing and publishing. It has also published "The Japan Style Sheet," a guide for the use of Romanized Japanese and other problems of usage involving Japanese in English texts. The group would naturally be a good source for inquiries on translation, publishing, interpreting, design/editorial work, etc.

SWET
2-19-15-808 Shibuya
Shibuya-ku, Tokyo 150

3. FCC (Forum for Corporate Communications)

The FCC is open to anyone in corporate communications businesses, whether Japanese or foreign, and is mainly for those in marketing, advertising, public relations, writing, editing, or translation services. FCC holds a monthly dinner meeting with speakers on various corporate communications topics, and has educational workshops, including some on how to market items in Japan and how to read annual reports.

Membership is 50% foreign and 50% Japanese.

The FCC can be contacted at (03) 433-3874.

## 4. The Foreign Correspondents' Club

The Press Club, as it is called, is a private club that was established in 1945 for foreign journalists stationed in Japan. However, the club admits non-journalist members as well.

Currently, there are 2,000 members, 450 of whom are journalists, the rest being associate members. The Club has two dining rooms, a media lounge, a library, and a clipping service for members.

Associate membership fees are quite hefty, a ¥450,000 entrance fee and a monthly fee of ¥13,700, but several small business members acknowledged the benefits of good business and press contacts.

The Foreign Correspondents' Club of Japan
Yurakucho Denki Bldg., 20th F.
1-7-1 Yurakucho
Chiyoda-ku, Tokyo 100
Tel: (03) 211-3161/7

# 14

# Helpful Organizations

## JETRO (JAPAN EXTERNAL TRADE ORGANIZATION)

JETRO is an organization funded by the Japanese government to promote exports to Japan. Therefore, most of the information disseminated by this entity is import/export oriented, rather than centered on domestic business. However, the list of publications offered by JETRO does include items that could be helpful to domestic businesses, such as market research studies and a book on setting up in Japan.

JETRO in Tokyo has a large reading room and copying facilities and all of its own publications on hand and for sale, as well as numerous other publications. In addition, the staff members are extremely helpful, speak excellent English, and are willing to answer questions business owners might have. (Some of the JETRO people were working in Japanese business or industry prior to employment there, so they can offer advice on the market from direct experience.)

JETRO has also coordinated "Made in U.S.A." fairs with the ACCJ to promote imports and has sent missions of buyers to the U.S. to scout for new products to import. However, the most valuable feature of the organization is its publication of comprehensive explanatory works on the Japanese market. Small entrepreneurs should utilize these works and the expertise of the JETRO staff (particularly since the latter is free of charge).

JETRO's hours: Monday–Friday 9:30 a.m.–5:00 p.m.
Saturday 9:30 a.m.–12:00 p.m.

JETRO
2-2-5 Toranomon
Minato-ku, Tokyo 105

International Communication Department      582-5521
Import Promotion & Cooperation Department 582-5543
Economic Information Department           582-5568

Information Service Department
    Business Library                      582-1775
    Standards Information Service Division 582-6270
    Investment Promotion Division         582-5571

Machinery & Technology Department         582-5579
Publications Department                   582-3518
Agriculture Department                    582-5580

## FOREIGN CUSTOMER LIAISON OFFICES

Several of the department stores in Tokyo, such as Seibu, Matsuya, and Isetan, have started a new service known as "foreign customer liaison offices." These act as consultants on the various services and products that foreign residents in Japan want but can't easily get due to language problems, lack of information or just plain unavailability.

How can these "liason offices" help small entrepreneurs? They offer these services: real-estate referral, furniture leasing, catering, gifting, locating hard-to-find items, customizing product promotion, you name it, and all at no charge.

Pamela Fields of Matsuya's "Gaigaisho" service emphasized that both large and small foreign companies take advantage of the free service because it saves time, effort, and money. Ms. Fields also made it clear that Matsuya's service is strictly for companies while Seibu's is primarily for individuals.

Gaigaisho
Matsuya Department Stores
3-6-1 Ginza
Chuo-ku, Tokyo 104
Tel: (03) 567-6672

I Club Service Counter
Isetan Department Stores
3-14-1 Shinjuku
Shinjuku-ku, Tokyo 160
Tel: (03) 356-4311

Foreign Customer Liaison Office
Yurakucho Seibu Department Store
2-5-1 Yurakucho
Chiyoda-ku, Tokyo 100
Tel: (03) 286-5482/3

## PEOPLE'S FINANCE CORPORATION *(KOKUMIN KIN'YŪ KŌKO)*

While some entrepreneurs had an extremely difficult road to travel before obtaining financing from this organization established by the Japanese government in 1949, Bunny Cramer of Witan Associates, with the help of her Japanese partner/guarantor, received a loan relatively easily and found People's "very helpful and friendly toward small business."

When this author called the organization and asked about guarantors and collateral requirements for foreign small businesses, the extremely "helpful and friendly" lady answering my questions said over and over that there is no policy of discrimination against foreigners. That is, loans require a guarantor, but he/she need not be Japanese, only financial capability and residence in Japan being necessary. Secondly, adequacy of collateral is decided on a case-by-case basis, but real estate is not always required, according to the organization's brochure.

Loans granted to foreign entrepreneurs in the past have been in an amount of ¥3–5 million, with a Japanese guarantor being necessary, despite the above representations. However, the People's organization may possibly be turning over a new leaf in relation to its policies on foreign small business loans and guarantors.

Service and trade businesses capitalized at less than ¥10 million with less than 50 employees, or individual entrepreneurs can apply for loans at People's. The money can be used to establish a business or to conduct operations already in existence. There is a limit on the amount to be borrowed (¥27 million), and the interest rate is currently 4.9%. Money borrowed for establishing a business must usually be repaid within 10 years—in specific cases, 15 years—and other money borrowed must be repaid within 5 years.

As to guarantors and collateral, only one guarantor is necessary for individual borrowers. A person other than a corporation's representative serving as guarantor is necessary for business borrowers. In cases where there is adequate security, a guarantor is not needed. This latter determination is made on a case-by-case basis.

Those seeking to establish a business as well as those already operating one may apply, although the opinion of foreign entrepreneurs "in the know" is that a year's track record is necessary before a foreign small business can get a loan.

The People's Finance Corporation (Main Office)
Koko Building
1-9-3 Otemachi
Chiyoda-ku, Tokyo
Tel: (03) 270-1361


**TOKYO CHAMBER OF COMMERCE** *(TŌKYŌ SHŌGYŌ KAIGISHO)*

For those who are fluent in Japanese, joining the Tokyo Chamber of Commerce is a wise investment for a variety of reasons. Unfortunately, since the Chamber publications—and proceedings—are in Japanese, new-to-Tokyo business people without the requisite language skills will not derive much benefit from this organization.

The Tokyo Chamber of Commerce, established over 100 years ago, has branch offices in each of the 23 wards of the city. One of the espoused characteristics of the organization is its goal of "internationalization," meaning communication with various Chambers of different countries, and promotion of international economic relations. The Tokyo Chamber also has several other spheres of activity, a major one being the promotion of small and medium business.

The small and medium business promotion activities are based on the presumption that these businesses are the backbone of the Japanese economy. To that end, the Chamber presents small and medium business proposals to national and local governments, and offers counseling on business operations and financing. Becoming a member of the Chamber provides you with, among other things, the following benefits:

1. access to the latest economic information (research materials, library, etc.);
2. economic counseling (specialty, trade, and business);
3. entrées to, and mediation services for, domestic and international trade;
4. educational seminars for employees and management;
5. private, individual consulting services in each of the 23 wards.

Joining the Chamber seems to be a relatively simple matter. At any of the 23 wards, membership can be applied for, but only by the following:

1. sole business owners or proprietors;
2. representatives of a company in business for at least six months.

An application for membership must be completed, which will then be submitted to the branch or the main office of the Chamber. The regular meeting of members on the second Thursday of the month will then confirm acceptance of the application and send notice of payment of fees. Once the fees are paid, membership status is conferred with proof of same being forwarded to the member. (This identification must be used to gain access to the various Chamber functions and services.)

The cost of membership is determined by one's categorization. A foreign individual proprietor or a foreign legal entity must apply for "special membership," which is ¥20,000 per year plus a ¥2,000 initiation fee. An individual who has a domestic corporation, however, will apply for corporate membership, which has an entrance fee of ¥2,000 and a yearly fee based on the company's capitalization amount. For example, a company capitalized at less than ¥5 million must pay a yearly fee in one installment of ¥15,000; a company capitalized at more than ¥5 million but less than ¥10 million pays a fee of ¥30,000 in two installments; a company capitalized at ¥10 million or more but less than ¥30 million pays a fee of ¥45,000 yearly in three installments.

The Chamber's small and medium business division is composed of a consulting section, financial services section—which provides introductions to other businesses—and a planning and research services section. The consulting service focuses on assisting with problems and offering planning services for financing, tax, general business operations, management, labor, modernization, etc. These services are all free of charge.

The most helpful feature of the Chamber is that it provides consultation sessions with lawyers, accountants, patent attorneys, trade consultants, small and medium business consultants, etc., on a no-charge basis. The experts are available at appointed times at the main office business consultation center, as well as at each of the 23 ward offices of the Chamber.

The Tokyo Chamber of Commerce (Main Office)
3-2-2 Marunouchi Tosho Bldg.
Chiyoda-ku, Tokyo 100
Tel: (03) 283-7500

## TOKYO CREDIT GUARANTEE ASSOCIATION *(TŌKYŌ SHIN'YŌ HOSHŌ KYŌKAI)*

This association was organized specifically to guarantee loans to those small and medium enterprises that do not have ample credit, collateral, or financing wherewithal, and it also makes guarantees for businesses in Tokyo that have been located at the same address and doing business for over one year. Either sole proprietors or companies may apply, but businesses must be capitalized at less than ¥10 million and employ less than 50 people.

The Credit Guarantee Association guarantees loans up to ¥10 million for up to ten years at the following annual rates of interest:

| | |
|---|---|
| under ¥1 million | 0.50% |
| ¥1 million–less than ¥3 million | 0.70% |
| ¥3 million–less than ¥5 million | 0.90% |
| ¥5 million and over | 1.00% |

Credit guarantees are provided for loans, *tegata* (promissory notes) issued by a business, and temporary overdrafts, and the Association automatically guarantees all loans made by the Japanese government, such as those of the People's Finance Corporation. A representative of a company is obliged to serve as a guarantor, along with the company, to ensure joint and several liability, and amounts of ¥10 million or less need no collateral.

As with the People's Finance Corporation situation detailed in the chapter on Financing, entrepreneurs have experienced repeated turndowns by the Association. However, Bunny Cramer of Witan Associates, who eventually got a loan from People's Finance, received a guarantee from the Association.

The Tokyo Credit Guarantee Association (Main Office)
Yasuda Seimei Yaesu Building, 6-8 Floors
2-6-17 Yaesu
Chuo-ku, Tokyo
Tel: (03) 272-2251

## TOKYO MUNICIPAL GOVERNMENT

The Tokyo Municipal Government offers a variety of financing packages in cooperation with the Credit Guarantee Association and designated financial institutions. Applicants can apply at, for example, the Credit Guarantee Association, the Tokyo Chamber of Commerce, or at any of the 23 ward offices.

As an example, there is a no-collateral, no-guarantor-required loan of up to ¥350,000 for individual proprietors with less than four employees. It must be repaid within five years at 4.9% interest. Another type of loan is the "small business loan" for ¥10 million or less to be repaid within five years at 5.4% which is also for businesses with less than five employees. The individual representative of the company must act as a guarantor in tandem with the company for joint and several liability purposes. Several other types of loans are also available.

The documents to be submitted when applying at the "loan window" of the above organizations include:

| | |
|---|---|
| Loan application form | (2 copies) |
| Credit guarantee consignment form and consignment contract | (1 copy each) |
| Loan performance information form | (1 copy) |
| Proof of seal of applicant and business representative | (1 copy each) |

Individuals must also submit income tax and enterprise tax receipts as well as two copies of recent tax returns. Corporate applicants must submit corporate registration papers, corporate and enterprise tax receipts, and two copies of the most recent balance sheet.

Dick Adler of Corton Trading was contacted by the Tokyo government through his Japanese bank and notified of the various loan programs available. In such a case, applications can be made directly through the bank to the government. Otherwise, application must be made at the above-mentioned institutions.

# 15

# Communication Services

## POSTAL SERVICES

The Japanese Post Office hours are as follows:

Tokyo International Post Office:

| | |
|---|---|
| Monday–Friday | 9:00 a.m.–7:00 p.m. |
| Saturday | 9:00 a.m.–5:00 p.m. |
| Sunday | Closed |

Branch Offices:

| | |
|---|---|
| Monday–Friday | 9:00 a.m.–5:00 p.m. |
| Saturday | 9:00 a.m.–12:30 p.m. |
| Sunday | Closed |

**Note:** On the second and third Saturday of the month, the Tokyo International Post Office is not open for savings account transactions; all small branch offices are completely closed on those days.

The Tokyo International Post Office
2-3-3 Otemachi
Chiyoda-ku, Tokyo 100
Tel: (03) 241-4891

## MAIL INFORMATION

Air mail and Japanese domestic express mail services are available on a 24-hour basis at the Tokyo International Post Office.

Bulk mail printed matter is handled only by the Tokyo, Yokohama, and other main branch offices, not small, local neighborhood branches.

Any post office will handle packages of up to 10 kilograms, whether insured or not, but packages over that weight that are to be insured can only be handled by a main branch.

There is a two-kilogram limit on items classified as "small packets."

### PARCEL/SMALL-PACKAGE DELIVERY SERVICES

There are several services that deliver packages and small parcels that are often conveniently located at, for example, your nearby 7-11. Yamato Un'yu *(takkyū bin)*, with a logo of two black cats, is open seven days a week, including holidays, and can usually deliver your item the next day. Akabō delivers packages on an individual basis, item by item, and calculates rates based on mileage plus the time it takes to pickup/load and unload/deliver. (The maximum weight that can be sent via Akabō is 350 kg, but there is no limit on the number of items.)

The Post Office small-package delivery service offers the convenience of home or office pickup. More than 10 items sent gives you a 10% discount and more than 100, a 25% discount. Proof of receipt can be sent to you via post card. The maximum size for a package (length × width × depth) is 150 cm. No dimension may be more than 100 cm.

### REGISTERED MAIL

The *genkin kakitome* (registered mail) service is a convenient and relatively inexpensive way to send payments domestically. (Another way is the automatic bank transfer, or *genkin furikomi,* costing ¥400–800 and taking from 1–3 days.) Up to ¥200,000 can be sent by registered mail.

When sending an amount of up to ¥10,000, the registered mail charge is ¥350. To every successive ¥5,000 increment sent, ¥10 is added. For example, a ¥15,000 remittance costs ¥360.

Messages can be included in the envelope, which costs ¥20. The ability to send a message is one advantage that the bank transfer system does not have.

## THE POSTAL SAVINGS SYSTEM

The Post Office offers three basic types of savings systems: the ordinary account, the time deposit (in six- and ten-month terms), and the monthly deposit system for salaried workers and old age pensioners. The postal savings system, like that of most banks in Japan, offers a cash-card service (especially convenient if you are outside of Tokyo, where your regular bank cash-card may not be usable), automatic payment transfer, and wire transfer systems as well as allowance for direct deposit of money from salary and/or bonus into postal accounts.

Loans can also be made through the postal savings system by using fixed-time deposits as security. The loans must be within 90% of the amount of the fixed-time deposit, and can be for up to ¥1 million. Loans must be repaid within one year of the day of the receipt of the money.

## INTERNATIONAL POSTAL REMITTANCE SERVICE

International postal money orders can be sent to 71 countries to pay for subscriptions, products purchased, membership fees, etc. Throughout Japan, 5,600 of the post offices provide this service, and 39 provide telegraphic transfer services.

There are two types of money orders. The first type is an ordinary money order for cash payment which is sent by air mail or by telegraph for more rapid payment. Messages can be sent with payment. The second type is an "international postal *giro*" for in-payments, if the payee has a "postal *giro*" account in Japan, or for transfers between Japanese and foreign postal *giro* account holders. Messages can also be sent with payment. The *giro* account holder can send money by air mail to the *giro* account abroad—the charge is ¥400 per transaction—or by telegraphic transfer.

A schedule of current charges (April 1988) for international postal money orders is as follows:

| Amount | Charge | |
| --- | --- | --- |
| | Ordinary | Inpayment |
| ¥10,000 | ¥ 800 | ¥ 600 |
| 10,001–50,000 | 1,000 | 700 |
| 50,001–100,000 | 1,200 | 800 |
| 100,001–200,000 | 1,500 | 1,000 |
| 200,001–300,000 | 2,000 | 1,500 |
| 300,001–400,000 | 2,500 | 2,000 |
| 400,001–500,000 | 3,000 | 2,500 |

**Note:** For amounts over ¥500,000, add ¥500 for each ¥100,000 increment. The above rates are also applicable to telegraphic charges for wire transfers.

Last, but not least, the most helpful service that the post office has initiated is a "foreign goods import system," which allows residents in Japan to pay for goods by international postal money order or international postal *giro* account transfer, and then to import them by mail.

## THE TELEPHONE

International telephone calls are handled by Kokusai Denshin Den-wa Corporation (KDD), which has an International Subscriber Dialing system (ISD) that is more economical than using an operator. (ISD charges are calculated every 6 seconds.) After joining ISD, you can make station-to-station calls directly from your home or office.

NTT (Nippon Telegraph and Telephone Corporation) is the authority that provides domestic telephone service and phone installation. NTT offers three types of business phones, the simplest being the "custom series." Model 308, for example, can be rigged for up to eight phone units, and a two-phone custom series costs ¥165,000 for installation, bond, and purchase of the phones. (Bonds cost ¥72,800 per line, the phone unit being ¥17,000 and the remainder going for installation charges.) The custom series can also be leased for ¥3,000 per month for seven years. (Phone lease contracts are on a seven-year basis.)

An alternative to the business phone is just to buy a regular, standard phone. The bond is ¥72,800/line, there is a ¥10,000 installation charge, and the phone can cost from ¥10,000–30,000. For a small business, the cheapest purchase rate of ¥92,000 for one phone may be better than paying ¥165,000 for a business phone system.

## FACSIMILES

A fax system can be purchased or leased, and prices vary widely for units (from ¥35,000–200,000), so you should "shop around." The installation costs are about ¥50,000 on average, but depending on the model, can run as low as ¥25,000 or as high as ¥70,000.

## SOME USEFUL NUMBERS

KDD
Tokyo Information Center
(all-day service) (03) 270-5111
Osaka Information Center
(all-day service) (06) 228-2300
ISD service (Tokyo) Dial 0057

NTT

Leasing and purchasing business
  phones (call in Japanese)                    (03) 501-5000

Telephone out of order                         Dial 113
Charge information system                       Dial 100
  (An operator can monitor your
    long-distance call within Japan
    and tell you the charge
    after you hang up.)
Overseas calls                                  Dial 0051

Directory information:
  Same area code as caller's              Dial 104
  Other area codes                          Dial 105
  From public telephones                   Dial 105

## INTERNATIONAL TELEX SYSTEM

KDD, Kokusai Denshin Denwa Corporation, also handles international telex matters. A telex unit can be purchased or rented, but in either case, the single installation fee is as follows:

| | |
|---|---|
| Contract charge | ¥ 300 |
| Line installation charge | 72,000 |
| Equipment installation charge | 30– 50,000 |
| Internal wiring charge | 70–100,000 |
| TOTAL | ¥172,300–222,300 |

KDD has three different telex units for rent, models ASR-11, ASR-12, and DSR-21. The ASR models are single units and cost ¥26,700 per month.

A Telestem DSR-32 model can be purchased in a two-part, seven-year payment system. Monthly payments are made for 1–5 years, whichever increment is most convenient. Then, a monthly fee is paid until the seven-year period ends. A monthly line and wiring charge is also mandatory.

As of January 1, 1988, automatic calls to the U.S. were ¥540 per minute and to Europe cost about ¥650 per minute.

## TELEGRAMS

International telegrams are also handled by KDD. Ordinary private telegrams may be written in plain or codal languages or both. There is a seven-word minimum.

Letter telegrams are made after 8:00 p.m. destination time following the date of sending in. The rates for these are one-half those for ordinary private telegrams, and they must have a minimum of 22 words.

Phototelegrams (which transmit pictorial materials) and typed or written ones are available for 40 different countries.

Urgent telegrams receive priority in transmission and delivery, but rates are twice those of ordinary private telegrams.

International telegrams are accepted at KDD's International Telegraph Offices and NTT's Telegraph Offices. Payments should be made in yen, but if prearranged with the addressee, a collect telegram can be sent.

KDD International Telegraph Office (Tokyo)
(03) 344-5151

# 16

# Business Directory

The following is a list of some of the business people interviewed for this book, and their product/service offerings:

**Adler, Dick** (American)
President, Corton Trading
  Co., Ltd.
4F, Yamaguchi Bldg.
1-12-8 Higashi Azabu
Minato-ku, Tokyo 106
Fax: (03) 587-1255
Tel: (03) 582-3371/2

Trading company—
specializing in high technology electronics, program
management, business
consulting

**Bliah, Richard** (French)
President, S.E.C. Co., Ltd.
Sankyo Hanzomon Palace 201
1-8-2 Hirakawa-cho
Chiyoda-ku, Tokyo 102
Tel: (03) 239-1339

Architectural, design, and
space-planning services

**Butler, Neil** (Australian)
Catchworld International
7F, Minami Aoyama A Bldg.
1-10-2 Minami Aoyama
Minato-ku, Tokyo 107
Fax: (03) 403-9105
Tel: (03) 423-1677

Trading in oils and com-
puters; business consulting,
tourism, investment and
marketing

**Connelly, Bob and Mary-Jane** (American)
International Technical Trading, Inc.
Takahashi Bldg.
22-28 Sanbancho
Chiyoda-ku, Tokyo 102
Fax: (03) 234-6915
Tel: (03) 234-6921

Import/export of products for water conservation, water pollution control, optics, housewares, sporting goods, technology transfer

**Cramer, Bunny** (American)
Witan Associates, Ltd.
Rm. 202, Daini Inoue Bldg.
2-17-13 Nihonbashi
Kayabacho
Chuo-ku, Tokyo 103
Fax: (03) 639-5498
Tel: (03) 666-5612

Corporate communications, including advertising, annual reports, audio-visual materials, corporate brochures, newsletters etc., in English and Japanese

**Daszkiewicz, Edmund** (British)
Managing Director
Procom Co., Ltd.
Yamamoto Bldg., 5F
3-30 Kioi-cho
Chiyoda-ku, Tokyo 102
Tel: (03) 234-0645

Computer systems and programs

**Doucet, Daniel** (French)
President
Epsilon Co., Ltd.
201 Shibuya Homes
2-1 Udagawa-cho
Shibuya-ku, Tokyo 150
Telex: J 32460AUDIODSN
Tel: (03) 477-7488

Import/export of foodstuffs
and agricultural produce

**Dunn, Michael** (British)
605 Mita Mansion
2-8-12 Mita
Minato-ku, Tokyo 108
Tel: (03) 451-8735

Fine Japanese art/antiques

**Gaynard, Valerie** (American)
President & Director
Interior Decor
Sono Bldg. 3F
1-7-10 Higashi Azabu
Minato-ku, Tokyo 106
Fax: (03) 586-9743
Tel: (03) 586-9741

Furniture leasing, sales, interior design, housing services
and business consulting

**Goldberzst, Jeanne** (French)
Style France
Ichiban-cho Central Bldg.
22-1 Ichiban-cho
Chiyoda-ku, Tokyo 100
Tel: (03) 234-0186

Import of French interior
decor and home furnishing
items and accessories

**Kennedy, Kerry** (Canadian)
President & Managing Director
Direct Marketing Services
  Japan, K.K.
Keiken Bldg., 3F
1-9-27 Kasuga
Bunkyo-ku, Tokyo 112
Fax: (03) 814-0368
Tel: (03) 814-6661

Creation, direct marketing, and planning of direct market research (mailing lists, response checks, catalogs, letter shopping and fulfillment services)

**Kininmonth, Hugh** (New Zealander)
205 Palatial Wako
1311-1 Shimo-Niikura
Wako-shi, Saitama-ken 351-01
Tel: (0484) 65-5573

Promotion of NZ goods, especially wool and sheepskin; agent for leather/fur producer; translation and interpretation

**Kuzui, Fran** (American)
Kuzui Enterprises, Inc.
Jonquil Building, 6F
33-1 Udagawa-cho
Shibuya-ku, Tokyo 150
Tel: (03) 464-5643

Film promotion, distribution, production, and entertainment representation and promotion

**Lloyd, Terrie** (New Zealander)
Linc Japan, Ltd.
705 Gloria Miyamasuzaka III
1-10-7 Shibuya
Shibuya-ku, Tokyo 150
Fax: (03) 498-7280
Tel: (03) 409-6510

English and Japanese language advertising; purchasing of space in Japanese and foreign magazines; import/export of computer hardware/ software

**Lyster, Reiko** (American)
President & Chief Executive
  Officer
Elle International Co., Ltd.
World Yotsuya Bldg., 6F
4-3-1 Yotsuya
Shinjuku-ku, Tokyo 160
Fax: (03) 359-3255
Tel: (03) 359-3251

Import of fine French cosmetics, perfumes and beauty items

**McDowell, John** (New
  Zealander)
Barker's Fruit Processors
104 Plaza Sun Tanaka
1-25-15 Narimasu
Itabashi-ku, Tokyo 175
Tel: (03) 977-7118

Import/promotion of NZ foodstuffs: fruit juice, fruit wine, processed seafood, jam, and preserves

**Meron, Aaron** (Israeli)
Montrive Co., Ltd.
Montrieve Bldg.
4-6-1 Shibakoen
Minato-ku, Tokyo 105
Tel: (03) 434-4891

Import, sale, and distribution of handbags and accessories

**Pachon, André** (French)
President, André Pachon K.K.
3-11-5 Roppongi
Minato-ku, Tokyo 106
Tel: (03) 404-0384 (Ile de
France); (03) 476-5025
(Restaurant Pachon)

French restauranteur (Ile de France and Restaurant Pachon)

**Pike, Graham** (British)
President
Pacific Marine K.K.
511 Yurakucho Bldg.
1-10-1 Yurakucho
Chiyoda-ku, Tokyo 100
Tel: (03) 214-5431

Technology transfer, shipping, trading, and consulting

**Regge, Claus** (German)
Network, Inc./Soundwork, Inc.
Tsurumaki Star House,
506-12 Waseda Tsurumaki-cho
Shinjuku-ku, Tokyo 162
Tel: (03) 205-4011

Advertising; technical translating and printing; imports; business consulting

**Spillum, Walt** (American)
President
Lindal Cedar Homes Japan/
    Danco Japan, Ltd.
202 Sunshine Suite,
Sanwa Bldg., No. 3
4-5-4 Iidabashi
Chiyoda-ku, Tokyo 102
Fax: (03) 234-4413
Tel: (03) 234-0597

Import/promotion and distribution of cedar homes, cedar timber, lumber and American wood products

**St. Gilles, Amaury** (American)
Amaury St. Gilles Contem-
    porary Fine Art
3-2-9 Ohi
Shinagawa-ku, Tokyo 140
Tel: (03) 775-2740

Contemporary Japanese ceramics and graphics; art agent for international artists and exhibits

**Stiebling, Klaus** (German)
Europe Art Co. Ltd.
Grace Nishiogi #103
3-2-15 Shoan
Suginami-ku, Tokyo 167
Tel: (03) 332-7346

Import of fine art, books, prints and portfolios from Europe for sale to Japanese dealers

**Thaler, Willi** (American)
President
Incubator International
C.P.O. Box 2154
Tokyo 100-91
Fax: (03) 586-2048
Tel: (03) 586-3421

Market entry service and representation

**Wetmore, Deborah J.**
(Canadian)
Managing Director
Wetmore Financial Programs, K.K.
Dai-Ichi Chojiya Bldg. 7F.
1-2-13 Shibadaimon
Minato-ku, Tokyo 105
Fax: (03) 432-1199
Tel: (03) 432-8850

Financial planning services

**Wilson, Chuck** (American)
Clark Hatch Physical Fitness
  Center
Azabu Towers
2-1-3 Azabudai
Minato-ku, Tokyo 106
Tel: (03) 584-4018/4092

Health and physical fitness consulting; fitness center operations

**Wouters, Dave** (American)
Wouters & Associates, Inc.
6-16-50 Roppongi
Minato-ku,Tokyo 106
Fax: (03) 423-7492
Tel: (03) 423-7491

Insurance planning; management consulting and market studies; joint venture analyses; executive search; direct representation; business establishment and retirement funding

**Yonamine, Jane** (American)
President
Wally Yonamine Co., Inc.
2nd Floor
4-11-8 Roppongi
Minato-ku, Tokyo 106
Tel: (03) 402-4001
      (03) 403-4687

Cultured pearls and fine jewelry

# Conclusion

Small foreign businesses in Japan have contributed to the vitality of both Japanese and overseas economies by creating a link between the two. It has been a difficult, often frustrating, and yet rewarding path for those business owners who have all cultivated the qualities listed at the outset of this book: perseverance, optimism, and adaptation.

To succeed in Japan, having the drive to be in business is a must, along with quality products or services that are competitive, knowledge of the marketplace, and presence over a number of years. By working in tandem with overseas suppliers and larger businesses—either foreign or Japanese—and serving both foreign and Japanese commercial spheres by importing, exporting, or providing services, the small foreign business can be a conduit for trade with Japan and Japan's trade with the world.

# Recommended Reading

1. *Gaijin Guide,* by Janet Ashby, published by the Japan Times, Tokyo, 1985.
   A handy reference book for those living in Japan without Japanese-language ability, or even for those who have it. This is a practical gathering of information on everyday life, from the post office to the restaurant.
2. *Taking on Japan,* published by Look Japan, Ltd., 1987.
   Here is a compilation of 12 articles on foreigners doing business in Japan originally published in *Look Japan* magazine. Since it is in a question-and-answer format, it makes easy reading.
3. *Business Tokyo* magazine, published monthly by Keizaikai Company, Ltd., Tokyo, has a monthly feature on foreign entrepreneurs in Japan. The magazine is ¥4,800 a year in Japan or $60.00 in the U.S.
4. *Doing Business in Japan,* by Mitchell F. Deutsch, published by New American Library, New York, New York, 1983. A former Sony employee walks you through the Japanese business world in a more accessible fashion than most other books of the same genre.
5. *Doing Business in Japan,* edited by Zentaro Kitagawa, published by Matthew Bender Publishers, New York, New York, 1980, Volumes 1–7 plus statutory indexes.
   This hefty 9-volume set is basically for legal practitioners, but is so comprehensive a work on the Japanese legal system and business law, and so simply written that "laymen" would probably benefit from browsing through sections on contracts, corporations, etc. It is expensive, so it is best to refer to it at

the Japan Foundation Library, which is a storehouse of information on Japan. Contact the Japan Foundation Library at (03) 263-4504.

6. *How to Do Business with the Japanese*, by Mark Zimmerman, published by Charles E. Tuttle Co., Tokyo, 1985.

   A certified Japan expert gives pointers on business à la Japan. While more "big-business" oriented and expositive than Mitchell Deutsch's book, which tends to be more "how-to," the abstractions are certainly relevant for all foreign business people in Japan.

7. *How to Do Business with the Japanese,* by Herbert F. Jung, published by the Japan Times, Tokyo, 1986.

   A very friendly approach to what and what not to do when trying to conduct business successfully in Japan, written by the former head of Bayer's Tokyo operations.

8. *Setting Up Enterprises in Japan,* compiled by the Bank of Japan, published by JETRO, 1983.

   A book that is basically for larger foreign-capital-affiliated enterprises but with parts pertinent to smaller companies. It is a comprehensive overview, yet is detailed enough to be a "how-to" book.

9. *Guide to Japanese Taxes, 1986-87,* by Yuji Gomi, published by Zaikei Shohosha, Tokyo, Japan.

   A very informative and useful guide to the tax system, which is updated yearly.

10. *Business Practices and Taxation in Japan,* by Takashi Kuboi, published by the Japan Times, Tokyo, 1988.

    A Japanese tax accountant with over 25 years of experience has written this extremely detailed but very easy-to-understand guide to business practices and taxation laws in Japan, including the new 1988 tax laws.

11. American Chamber of Commerce in Japan's *Journal* magazine occasionally does an issue on small business in Japan, the most

recent being the January 1985 issue. Back copies are available at ¥700 each from the ACCJ. Write to:

ACCJ, Publications Department,
7th floor, Fukide No. 2 Bldg.,
4-1-21 Toranomon, Minato-ku, Tokyo 105

12. JETRO publications
    The Japan External Trade Organization (JETRO) publishes marketing studies, business information, a monthly magazine called *Focus Japan*, and a helpful series called "Keys to Success in the Japanese Market" (1980–84), as well as a host of other publications. The organization has compiled a list of its works. Their address is:

    JETRO
    Publications Department
    2-2-5 Toranomon
    Minato-ku, Tokyo 105
    Tel: (03) 582-3518

13. *MIPRO Monitoring Survey,* published by MIPRO (Manufactured Imports Promotion Organization).
    This newsletter published by an affiliate of the Ministry of International Trade & Industry lists results of feasibility and marketability surveys of foreign products in Japan. In the past 18 months, 13 items have been surveyed, and MIPRO plans to conduct similar surveys on six products per year, free of charge, which will be published in the newsletter.

    MIPRO
    World Import Mart Bldg., 6th Floor
    3-1-3 Higashi Ikebukuro
    Toshima-ku, Tokyo 170
    Tel: (03) 988-2791

14. **Newsletter** put out by the Joint Japan-America Chambers Cooperation Committee, edited and published by Japan/Tokyo Chambers of Commerce & Industry.

This newsletter is a compilation of unofficial translations of original Japanese articles on various developments in the Japanese market, including, for example, the increase in direct mail, revision of standards for food and food additives, problems of distribution, etc. The newsletter is available to members of the ACCJ for ¥3,000/half-year, since it is being published on an experimental basis. Those who are not ACCJ members may be able to get a free copy, so write to or call:

 Japan Chamber of Commerce
 3-2-2 Marunouchi, Tosho Bldg.
 Chiyoda-ku, Tokyo 100
 Tel: (03) 283-7867

15. U.S. Department of Commerce Market Research Studies and Information.

The IMR (international market research) and CMS (country market survey) are market research studies by independent firms funded by the U.S. Department of Commerce. The former is a lengthy, detailed analysis of a specific area, and costs $100–$300 per survey, but can be found on file at the American embassy in the Commercial Library. The latter is an overview of Japanese market conditions updated yearly, is 10–20 pages long, costs about $10, and is also on file at the embassy.

A list of support organizations and consultants for the Japanese market is available for ¥5,000 and there is a paper on establishing a business in Japan costing ¥3,000. There are 24 different sector analysis studies or post-commercial action plans also available.

While most of the information is for manufacturers and exporters, the market research information is especially helpful to get a grasp on the Japanese market in a specific area.

# Index